Ta

Introduction

Duolingo English Exam

Introduction to this book:

The Duolingo English Test is a quick way of establishing a person's 'realistic' English proficiency. There are both 'good' and 'bad' points to the administration of this test. Obviously, one advantage is that it takes approximately an hour to do and 2 days to receive your results. However, much of the test is 'marked' or 'evaluated' by an algorithm developed by way of Artificial Intelligence (AI), which can be problematic with regard to speaking–especially in areas of dialect, rhythm, and intonation. Also, the test is slightly interactive in that there are 3 different levels of questions that are automatically scored; so if a test-taker scores 'high' on a level 1 question, they can be assured the next question will 'jump' to a level 2 question, which is slightly more difficult. Likewise, if the test-taker scores 'high' again on a level 2 question, the AI will ensure the test-taker moves to a level 3 task question.

There are 15 different scored tasks on this exam, some of which can be repeated as many as 6 times, and 2 <u>unscored</u> sample questions (Speaking - Video, and Writing) that are sent along to the college, university, or employer the test-taker has applied to.

Tasks Scored by an Algorithm	Automatically Graded Tasks
1. Read Aloud	1. Read and Complete
2. Write About the Photo	2. Read and Select
3. Speak about the Photo	3. Listen and Select
4. Read, Then Write	4. Listen and Type
5. Listen, The Speak	5. Complete the Sentences
6. Read, Then Speak	6. Complete the Passage
	7. Highlight the Answer
	8. Identify the Idea
	9. Title the Passage

The Complete Duolingo

The rationale behind *The Complete Duolingo* is simple: If the test-taker understands how and in what way they are being tested, then this exam will prove to be much easier than anticipated. Because the Duolingo exam uses AI and has a massive database to choose questions from, there is no way to predict which questions will be chosen or how many times a question will be repeated. So, the best way for test-takers to control their outcome or score is to be knowledgeable of the English language skills (found in Part 1 of this text) and follow the techniques and methods for the different tasks (in Parts 2 and 3) as a way of making this exam easier, less stressful, and produce the highest possible scores.

This text foregrounds the 'Appendix', which is a different approach from many tests. Here it is hoped that test-takers review this section to come up to speed on the different Parts of Speech, Sentence Structure, or the types of sentences that should vary in your writing, Verb tenses, 'Paragraph form', and Listening skills. Further, the Online Resources in Part 7 give websites where you can practice these skills as well.

We place the Appendix in this prominent position in the text (Part1) because the Duolingo Exam shifts so quickly from task to task in different skills that it is deemed necessary 'to know' these skills in the Appendix because there are not long periods on the exam for Reading, Writing, Speaking, and Listening. The longest period for any task is 7 – 8 minutes, but you have to complete 6 reading tasks in that period. So, test-takers need to shift quickly from different skill sets and, therefore, need to be prepared.

Most Important

To score well, a test-takers MUST know the Paragraph form well because it will help in Writing, Speaking, and even Reading tasks. This is the 'perfect' skill to master for this exam because it allows you to recognize a topic sentence and its 2 parts, the topic and controlling idea, and then answer quickly. Oral answers to questions should follow this same form as writing since the algorithm will 'grade' all of the speaking and writing parts. This is extremely important to notice now – about the algorithm – because your responses for Speaking and Writing MUST be ORGANIZED. The paragraph form organizes these 2 types of responses for you, so you will score very high marks if you follow this form. Likewise, signal words in the paragraph form are important, too, because they tell the algorithm you are organized: words like 'however', 'but', 'on the other hand' **to show contrast**, or words for **sequenced responses**: 'first', 'second', 'next', 'finally', or words that help you **elaborate an argument**, like 'in addition' and 'furthermore', or words to add **importance or emphasis**, like 'in other words', 'that is', or 'by way of explanation'. These 'signal words' signal to your audience when you write or speak, but they also signal to the 'grading engine' algorithm that your response is organized.

What is the Duolingo Exam?

The Duolingo exam is 'adaptive', like the American Accuplacer Test, which means if you get answers correct, then the next test question will be slightly more difficult – towards a Level 3 question. Likewise, if the test-taker gets a question wrong, the next question will be slightly easier–towards a Level 1 question. In this way, through the 15 graded tasks on this exam (some questions are relative to the exam-makers only and are not scored), the algorithm winnows out a score in multiples of 5 to a maximum score of 160 points. The Duolingo website suggests the test is complete when its 'grading engine' is 'confident' of the test-taker's score.

Where is it acceptable for college or university entrance?

The Duolingo exam has been around since 2016, but it really took off during the Covid Crisis as students could not take any of the traditional exams to enter college or university (IELTS, PTE-A, CELPIP, or TOEFL), so the need for an online test that can be done in your home was necessary. This exam is accepted in most Canadian and American schools now, but this might change with the retreat of Covid and a return to the 'acceptance' of the more traditional exams mentioned above. However, schools are businesses in one sense, so the Duolingo exam may remain popular. It is advised that potential undergraduate students check Duolingo's 'acceptability' at the tertiary school they wish to attend.

Some Similarities and Differences between the traditional and Duolingo exams

All English second language proficiency exams will monitor a person's Speaking, Listening, Reading, and Writing skills; however, each exam varies its form to get results. For example, IELTS will have face-to-face Speaking with a human examiner and offer paper exams in some places. Other exam types, like Duolingo, will have you speak into a microphone and record yourself. A significant change from traditional exams is that Duolingo will change from a

Reading to a Listening to a Writing task in different orders and in a short period of time. Tradition exams have long periods of time for Speaking, Listening, Reading, and Writing parts on their exams, but Duolingo moves quickly between its tasks, and this may cause problems for some test-takers if they are not prepared for these hyper movements.

However, the Duolingo exam is much quicker than other exams (approximately 1 hour) because there are no long texts to read (usually only a paragraph or 2), no long audio clips to listen to (5-7 seconds at most) or long writing parts that extend to an hour long. Rather, the reading and listening tasks are short, and the writing parts are a maximum of 1 to 5 minutes in length.

Finally, and perhaps the most helpful point for many, Duolingo can be taken conveniently in your home, and the price is far less expensive than the other traditional English proficiency exams.

Preparation is critical; so, know the Rules, too.

Since there is less time between tasks and many of the tasks (9) are automatically graded, task-takers have to prepare. Obviously, the best place to start is the Duolingo website,

https://englishtest.duolingo.com/home , where you can 'Try the Test' (a 15-minute version) as many times as you like. This is necessary because you can get a feel for the shifting between skills and tasks and any other problems that may hinder you with this exam form. Test-takers should work on their English skills; their proficiency in Speaking, Writing, Reading, and Listening. The Appendix (Part 1) reviews all of the necessary skills, and there are methods and tips for every task within Parts 2 and 3 with many practice questions that are answered in Part 4. Also, there are sections for Vocabulary (Part 6), Topical questions for Speaking and Writing (Part 5) as well as Online resources (Part 7) to practice English language skills. Again, you are advised to know proper Paragraph form, especially a topic sentence, because this will assist on most every Speaking and Writing task, and help you analyze Reading tasks accurately. Thus, test-takers should practice topic sentences in conversations and use them when writing. Further, try to 'notice' while reading, how every writer uses a topic sentence in their writing – if you 'notice', it is one of the greatest keys to learning a second language (see Schmidt's Noticing Hypothesis) https://onlinelibrary.wiley.com/doi/abs/10.1002/9781118784235.eelt0086.pub2

The Rules

The rules for the Duolingo exam are very important. You will take the test online from your own home, but you cannot interact with anyone else in the room, wear ear/ headphones or look offscreen!

Your head with your eyes down or looking forward must always be in the 'screen area' of your camera; thus, if you turn away for an extended period of time, the Duolingo examiners may cancel your test results, considering them to be fraudulent. Also, test-takers cannot take any notes or hold a pen at any time during the exam. This seems to be an odd rule as taking notes allows a person to organize their thoughts, but this is not allowed. Again, Duolingo test-takers really need to practice so as not to get tripped up at their computer during the test. The rules can be found on the Duolingo website, but some of the important rules are found below.

You need:

a government-issued photo ID

a quiet well-lit room

one hour of uninterrupted time (no distractions – the doorbell may ring, but you cannot move from your place for the exam)

a computer with a camera, positioned so your head is clearly in the frame (for the entire exam)

an internet connection and a well-matched browser (there are rules for the browser as well so that it demonstrates the test-taker is not cheating in any way)

Exam Overview

called '**Onboarding**' – **Estimated time 5 minutes**

CHECK: Computer + Identification + Review of test Rules

The Duolingo Exam - **Estimated time 45 minutes**

Adaptive testing for 45 minutes through Random selection from their Speaking, Listening, Reading, and Writing tasks.

Or the Duolingo Exam ends before the 45-minute mark because the 'grading engine' has enough information.

3. Writing and Speaking Samples (Video) - **Estimated time 10 minutes**

Writing Sample is 3 – 5 minutes in length.

Speaking Video is 1- 3 minutes in length.

*Note -You can see both of these Sample tasks after the exam is complete.

After the Duolingo Exam

Usually, within 48 hours, a test-taker will be notified by email of their scores, or he or she can frequently check their homepage on the Duolingo site. You may take the test two times within 3 days. Sometimes, test-takers experience technical problems, but you are allowed to take 2 'certified' tests within 30 days, regardless of any problems; hence, interestingly enough, there is a button on most of the exam tasks that says, 'Quit test', perhaps due to test-takers having computer issues or another form of difficulty.

Duolingo Scores vs. The CELPIP and IELTS exams

Duolingo	CELPIP (varies slightly with particular skill S, L, R, &W)	IELTS	TOEFL iBT	CEFR (Common European Framework Reference)
75 - 80	5	5.0	35 - 46	B1
85 - 90	6	5.5	47 - 58	B1
95 - 100	7	6.0	59 - 69	B1/B2
105 -110	8	6.5	70 - 81	B2
115 - 120	9	7.0	82 - 92	B2
125 - 130	9.5	7.5	93 - 103	B2/C1
135 - 140	10	8.0	104 - 112	C1
145 - 150	10.5	8.5	112 - 116	C1

155 - 160	11		9.0	117 - 119	C1/C2

Most North American schools ask for a score above 120 on the Duolingo exam. Scores, measured by increments of 5 points, can range from 10 – 160 on the Duolingo exam.

By all means visit the Duolingo website for FAQs: https://englishtest.duolingo.com/faq

or you can email englishtext-support@duolingo.com for help.

Be Test Wise

This exam will introduce many different tasks that are unique to the Duolingo exam over the traditional exams. For example, a 1 to 3-minute Sample video, a Speaking task, and a 3-to-5-minute Sample Writing task that go ungraded but are passed along to university, college, or employer administrations. These two 'sample' parts can really help your application because it gives the college, university, or even a potential employer a glimpse of the test-taker using their productive skills – speaking and writing.

Generally, the exam tasks require you to:

1. Record your spoken responses to a spoken question (Listen to a Question)

2. Selecting 'Real' words from a list of 'real' and 'made up' words

3. Likewise, listening to spoken words and decide if they are 'real' or 'made up' words

4. Filling in missing letters for words in a text

5. Typing a statement or question that you hear (Listen and Type)

6. Look at a picture and describe it in spoken words; describe it written words

7. Writing a minimum of 50 words in response to written question

8. Record yourself reading a written sentence

Frequency of Duolingo Tasks	Task Maximum on Exam
1. Read and Complete	3 times – 3 levels
2. Read and Select	3 times – 3 levels (15 words)
3. Listen and Select	3 times – 3 levels (9 words)
4. Listen and Type	4 -5 times
5. Read Aloud	3 times – 3 levels
6. Write About the Photo	3 times – 3 levels
7. Speak About the Photo	3 times – 3 levels
8. Read, Then Write	3 times – 3 levels
9. Read, Then Speak	3 times – 3 levels
10. Listen, Then Speak	3 times – 3 levels (9 words)
11. Complete the Sentences	3-6 times – 3 levels
12. Complete the Passage	3-6 times
13. Highlight the Answer	3-6 times
14. Identify the Idea	3-6 times
15.Title the Passage	3-6 times
16. Speaking Sample (not scored)	Maximum 1
17. Writing Sample (not scored)	Maximum 1

Note*: The algorithm (grading engine) with stop individual tasks when it has reached a 'confidence' in a grade, so a test-taker may not complete 4, 5, or 6 rotations on an individual task.

GENERAL TIPS

- **Answer every question.**
- **Use all the time allotted (if you finish a task early, you can rest!)**
- **Leave time to check your answers where necessary.**

Part 2

The APPENDIX

Many of the Duolingo tasks on this exam are related to major skills in the English language and 'background schemata' (or what the test-taker already knows and brings to the exam) that the test-taker should know. Some of the skill is grammatical, and other skills such as 'Paragraph form', Parts of Speech, Reading Skills, and Sentence Structure, should be understood before the test-taker begins their final review for the Duolingo exam. For example, by knowing the proper Paragraph form a test-taker will be prepared to answer the four Duolingo writing tasks, the Writing Sample, and several of the Reading tasks because understanding that a topic sentence = topic + a controlling idea is essential to scoring high on this exam. A 'controlling idea' is something the test-taker 'writes', whereas when a test-taker reads a passage, the controlling idea becomes the 'main idea' (generally) of a passage. Essentially, if you know what you are looking for in a paragraph – topic sentence, support sentences, detail or examples, or a conclusion – 'or how to construct a paragraph properly' - many of the tasks on the Duolingo exam can be understood in a few seconds and then completed on time; in this way, so much of the struggle is eliminated. However, you will have to practice all 17 tasks on this test, so you will be completely prepared. Why be prepared, you ask? Well, because all parts of this exam are timed, you need to be prepared – you need to immediately recognize what the task is asking of you, so you save time, not panic, and lower stress to a point where you can concentrate and be confident in your responses.

We ask that test-takers review and practice (practice included below) these English language skills and return to them when necessary, as the proceeding Parts of *The Complete Duolingo* will refer back to these skills.

1. Parts of Speech

- Parts of Speech, especially nouns, verbs, adjectives, and adverbs, are extremely important to know.

8 Parts of speech (articles a, an, and 'the' are not included in this set)

Parts of Speech	Definition	Types
Nouns	a person, place, thing	+ Gerunds and infinitives
Verbs	Action/ non-action or stative	Count and non-count
Adjectives	modify a noun	-ing and ed endings; a single word
Adverbs	Modify a verb, adverb, or adjective	Adverbs of time/frequency/degree/ manner/place/affirmation
Pronouns	Substitute for nouns	Subject/object/possessive adjectives/possessive/ self-reflexive
Prepositions	links nouns/pronouns/phrases	place/time/objects/people
Conjunctions	A word used to connect clause or sentences or to coordinate words in the same clause	Coordinating Subordinating
Interjections	Use of emotion	Exclamation marks!

Note:

1. Adjectives modify nouns; Nouns = persons, places, things, and ideas.
2. Adverbs can modify adjectives, verbs, and other adverbs.
3. Verbs as either action or nonaction (stative) and either transitive or intransitive while
4. Nouns are persons, places, things, or ideas.

Parts of speech are important not only for noting which part of speech is being used but also for 'the form' or the suffix added to the root word being used.

Pronouns:

Subject	Object	Possessive Adjectives	Possessive	Self - Reflexive
I	me	my	mine	myself
you	you	your	yours	yourself
he	him	his	his	himself
she	her	her	hers	herself
it	it	its	X	itself

Plural

We	us	our	ours	ourselves
You	you	your	yours	yourselves
they	them	their	theirs	themselves

Test-takers should be able to recognize and use all of these forms of Pronouns in a sentence.

Morphology is the term linguists use to discuss the changes in meaning of a root word as prefixes and suffixes are added to them. On the Duolingo Exam it is important to note the changes that occur to the meanings of words as suffixes are added to the end of a word to change meanings, especially in the *Read and Complete* task (rarely are prefixes used). Again, this might inform Level 2 or 3 parts to several tasks on the exam.

For example, observe the different suffixes added to the end of these words:

Noun	Verb	Adjective	Adverb
culture	X	cultural	culturally
distinction	distinguish	distinct	distinctly
generation	generate	generated	generationally
investment	invest	invested	X
link	link	X	X
negation	negate	X	X
pity	pity	X	X
signal	signal	signal	X

Note: Suffixes indicate a word's part of speech, or its meaning, or both.

For example, the word distinction as found in the table above tells you just buy its ending 'tion' that it is a noun.

The professor has served his country with great <u>distinction</u> (noun).

Likewise, the rest of the word forms can be used in similar fashion.

The professor has <u>distinguished</u> himself in his field of study. (Past participle in a perfect tense)

The professor has a <u>distinct</u> understanding of his scientific field. (Adjective modifying understanding).

The professor <u>distinctly</u> understands his field of study (adverb modifying the verb understands).

In each of the examples above the different suffixes of the word have several different grammatical uses and several different meanings.

Word form	Meaning
Distinction (noun)	- a difference or contrast; an excellence that separates one form others
Distinguish (verb)	- recognize or treat someone or something as different
Distinct (adjective)	- recognizably different in nature from something else
Distinctly (adverb)	- in a way that is readily or clearly unique

Different suffix endings are crucial to understand when you are confronted with a blank and possible word options.

Here are <u>some</u> typical adjective suffixes: (google 'adjectives' for a more comprehensive list)

Adjective suffixes	Common adjectives
- ible	delectable, irresistible, permissible, tangible
- ed	related, rounded, biased, disinterested, occupied
- ent	salient, incoherent, independent, pertinent
- al	royal, spiritual, original, emotional, vital, colossal
- cal	logical, critical, crucial, principal, central
- ing	shocking, touching, appetizing, striking, leading
- ant	pliant, relevant, significant, important
- able	sustainable, remarkable, retainable, teachable
- ful	wonderful, pitiful, youthful, harmful, resentful
- ious	delicious, precious, luscious, sagacious,

- Adverbs can be easily identified by their 'ly' ending in most cases.
- However, there a several words that end in 'ly' that are adjectives, such as: lively, leisurely, early, chilly, beastly

costly, cowardly, crassly, deadly, early, elderly, enormously, fatherly, friendly, gentlemanly, ghastly, godly, greatly, heavenly, holy, homely, humanly, leisurely, lively, lonely, lovely, manly, masterly, miserly, monthly, motherly, nightly, poorly, portly, priestly, princely, saintly, scholarly, shapely, silly, stately, timely, ugly, ungainly, unruly, unsightly, unseemly, unworldly, vastly, weekly, worldly, yearly.

Some typical verb suffixes:

Verb suffixes	Examples
- ify	beautify, clarify, identify
- ate	complicate, dominate, irritate
- ise/ize	economise, realize, industrialize (s or z)
- en	harden, soften, shorten

Luckily, are few suffixes for verbs, so they can be quickly identified by there place in a sentence (S+V + O (or DO)) or by their inherent meaning.

Finally, noun suffixes are many. Here, again, is a general list of noun suffixes:

Common Noun Suffixes	Examples
- age	baggage, mileage, postage
- al	arrival, deferral, revival
- ance or ence	prominence, deliverance, insistence
- dom	freedom, fiefdom, kingdom
- ee	employee, trainee
- er/or	worker, director, player
- hood	neighbourhood, fatherhood, childhood
- ism	truism, capitalism, socialism
- ist	perfectionist, capitalist, trombonist
- ity/ty	piety, equality, cruelty
- ment	government, firmament, parliament
- ness	happiness, selfishness, usefulness
- ry	rivalry, robbery, ministry

-	ship	friendship, membership
-	sion/tion/xion	nation, pollution, complexion

Practice and More Understanding

What is context?

It is the sentences around a word.

You can learn a lot about a word from its context.

- You can learn the Part of Speech
- You can learn the meaning of a word.

For example:

Mary's birthday is next week. Her mother is planning a party and she has already though of a cake she would like to make for her. Her boyfriend is going to buy her a new (1) _____.

Choose a word from the box below to complete the sentence above.

far away	neighbour	remember	shoe	watch	exceptional

(2) What is the Part of Speech for the missing word? _____.

Only a **noun** can follow 'buy her a new'

The nouns in the box above are – neighbour, show, and watch.

You need to choose a word that would be something to buy for a birthday present (using your background knowledge or schemata).

You can't buy a neighbour, nor would you give a person a shoe for their birthday, so 'watch' has to be the correct answer.

English syntax most often moves from Subject to Verb to Object (subjects and object are usually nouns and/ pronouns, and adjective and adverbs find their places between them). On the Duolingo exam, you should have some practice at this for *Complete the Sentence.*

Practice:

Complete the sentences below with words from the box.

ran	sent	different	easy	rules	worked	young	got	difficult

Barry's father was very poor and uneducated, and Barry was unhappy with him. At the age of twelve, Barry (1)_____ away from home. The police found him and (2)_____ him to a special home. Then they (3)_____ in touch with his mother, Mary Sheldon, and he went to live with her in Austin, Texas. Life with her mother was not (4) _____ for Barry. She was very (5) _____ from his father. She had a lot of (6) _____ .

1. Part of speech – verb - ran

2. Part of speech – verb - sent

3. Part of speech – verb - got

4. Part of speech – adjective - easy

5. Part of speech – adjective – difficult

6. Part of Speech – noun - rules

More Parts of Speech Practice

Practice these Word Families – use a dictionary if you have to (answers not provided)

Noun	Verb	Adjective	Adverb
	think		
success			
		general	
			really
		separate	
		special	
difference			
	open		
		simple	
est			

Verb Tenses you should know

Any person can get by with the essential Verb Tenses of Simple Present, Simple Past, Simple Future, and Present Continuous or Progressive. However, all 12 are presented in this chart.

	Past	Present	Future*
Simple	I lived in Singapore.	I live in Singapore.	I will live in Singapore.
Continuous	I was living in Singapore	I am living in Singapore	I will be living in Singapore
Perfect	I had lived in Singapore.	I have lived in Singapore.	I will be living in Singapore.
Perfect Continuous	I had been living in Singapore.	I have been living in Singapore.	I will have been living in Singapore.

Passive Verb Forms

The Passive Voice is used when it does not matter 'who' does the action. On the Duolingo test, when a test-taker writes it should always be in the Active form.

For example.

Active Sentence: John washed the car yesterday.

Passive: The car was washed yesterday (by John).

- Note: An active sentence means the 'subject' (John) is responsible for the 'action', whereas in the passive statement, we do not know 'who' performs the action.

The Passive may be used *Read and Complete* task, for example, at Level 3. But it will not be used at Level 1 and 2.

For more information on 'the Passive Voice' and Verb Tenses please use this link:

https://www.youtube.com/watch?v=pxbQ2U3Uuv0&t=495s

or search Anglo-link on YouTube for verb tenses as well.

Test-takers should be aware of the Passive Voice but it is not critical to scoring high on the Duolingo exam.

3. Sentence Structure

On the Duolingo Exam 'sentence structure awareness' is important for the longer writing tasks because the algorithm will notice the 'variations' used in the types of sentences and award consistently higher scores.

Below are the basic types of sentences and how they are used in sentences

(1) A clause always has a subject (S) and a verb (V). **RULE**

For example: (S) John (V) runs to the store – this is an independent clause. It is called an independent clause because it is a complete thought. An independent clause is a sentence.

(2) There are four (4) types of sentences in the English language and they all can be used in the written tasks on the PTE exam.

1. Simple sentences
2. Compound Sentences
3. Complex Sentences
4. Compound-Complex sentence

Simple Sentences:

A simple sentence may be complete in any of the following 4 forms:

1. One Subject and one Verb; John runs to the store. (S + V + complement)

2. One Subject and two Verbs; John walks and runs to the store. (S+ VV + complement) [***used specifically in the 3rd sentence of the introductory paragraph – see Write Essay].

3. Two Subjects and one Verb; John and Rajeev walk to the store. (SS+V + complement)

4. Two or more Subjects and two Verbs; John and Rajeev walk and run to the store.   (SS +VV + complement)

Compound Sentences

A Compound Sentence joins at least two independent clauses joined as a single sentence.

These are independent clauses or complete sentences that are joined together; hence, they are made 'compound'. These can be used throughout the written parts of the exam but especially in Summarize Written Text where you usually summarize cause and effect essays.

You can join independent clauses in 3 ways:

1. Coordinating conjunctions (the most common)

2. Conjunctive Adverbs (useful to know when rewriting the Write Essay prompt)

3. A semicolon (the two independent clauses must be related across the semicolon)

Coordinating Conjunctions: (the first and most commonly used way to form a sentence)

These are typically called 'FANBOYS' as this is an acronym for the coordinating conjunctions: For, And, Nor, But, Or, Yet, and So. Each word has a specific function as a conjunction (see the chart below)

Coordinating Conjunctions	Function (*note the comma placement after the first independent clause)
For	introduces a reason: I like math, for I like numbers.
And	introduces an equal idea: I like football, and I enjoy cricket.
Nor *Note: the question form after ', nor do I enjoy...'	introduces two negatives: I don't like swimming, nor do I enjoy bungee jumping.
But	introduces an opposing idea: I like watching films, but I don't like going to the theatre.
Or	offers a choice: We can out to dinner, or we can visit your sister.
Yet	used like 'but', however, offers a surprise: I like pizza, yet I do not like cheese.
So	introduces a result: I passed the test, so I feel good.

Conjunctive Adverbs: (the 2nd way to join independent clauses to form a sentence)

Conjunctive adverbs offer a similar function, just as the coordinating conjunctions do above, but are considered more formal (see the revised Chart below)

Coordinating Conjunctions and their corresponding Conjunctive Adverbs	Function (*note the different use of punctuation involving conjunctive adverbs – a semicolon and a comma)
For (Note: 'for' is not commonly used anymore; nowadays, people use 'because' in a dependent clause more often)	introduces a reason: I like math because I like numbers. · See dependent clauses
And Adverbs: in addition, furthermore, besides, also, moreover	introduces an equal idea: I like football; in addition, I enjoy cricket.
Nor	introduces two negatives: I don't like swimming, nor do I enjoy bungee jumping.
But - Adverbs: in contrast, on the other hand, on the contrary	introduces opposing ideas: I like watching films; on the other hand, I don't like going to the theatre.
Or Adverb: otherwise, instead, alternatively	offers a choice: We can out to dinner; otherwise, we can visit your sister.
Yet Adverbs: however, nevertheless, still, nonetheless	used like 'but', however, offers a surprise: I like pizza; nevertheless, I do not like cheese.
So Adverbs: as a result, consequently, therefore, hence, thus,	introduces a result: I passed the test; therefore, I feel good.
** 'for example' and 'for instance' are often used as conjunctive adverbs.	Many people must score higher than 79 on the PTE; for example, you will get extra points

	toward your immigration status in Australia if you do so.
To add an explanation: in other words, that is	Classical music is pleasing; in other words, this type of music is enjoyable.
To make a strong statement: indeed, in fact	Quantum computer technology may be revolutionary; indeed, research is on-going around the world.

Semicolons: (the 3rd way to independent clauses to form a sentence)

If two independent clauses are related, then a semicolon can be used to join them.

For example:

I like math; I like numbers.

I like watching films; I don't like going to the theatre.

I like pizza; I do not like cheese.

We can out to dinner; we can visit your sister.

Note: in each sentence above the two independent clauses are related, so a semicolon can be used to join them. Coordinating Conjunctions and Conjunctive Adverbs work to give the reader a 'function' or a way of understanding the relation between independent clauses. A semicolon, on the other hand, assumes the reader understands the relationship presented in each independent clause

Complex Sentences:

Complex sentences must have an independent clause and at least one (or more) dependent clause. **RULE** A dependent clause is written with a subordinate conjunction (see list below).

In the following examples, the dependent clauses are underlined:

1.   I like music because I like to dance.
2.   Although some people like to dance, other people do not like dancing.

3.   <u>Although some people like to dance</u>, other people do like dancing <u>because it involves moving to a beat.</u>

4.   <u>Although some people like to dance because it involves moving to the beat</u>, other people do not like dancing.

5.   Some people do not like dancing <u>although other people like to dance, because it involves moving to a beat.</u>

In (1), the independent clause is 'I like music', and this is joined to the dependent clause with the subordinate conjunction 'because'. Please note that 'Because I like to dance' is NOT an independent clause simply since a subordinate conjunction precedes the clause 'I like to dance'. The subordinate conjunction is the only 'word' that distinguishes an independent clause (IC) from a dependent clause (DC).

In (2), the dependent clause (DC) 'Although some people like to dance' precedes the independent clause (IC) with itself and a comma. As a rule, a dependent clause may precede or follow an independent clause. There is no punctuation needed between clauses if the independent clause is written first: [IC DC]. However, when the dependent clause is written first, there must be a comma before the independent clause [DC, IC].

In (3), the dependent clause (DC) 'Although some people like to dance' precedes the independent clause with itself and a comma, and another dependent clause 'because it involves moving to a beat'. As a rule, you form these types of complex sentences in any form: [DC IC DC – as in (3)], [DC, DC, IC – as in (4)], or [IC DC, DC]

Top 51 Subordinate conjunctions

1. after	18. if then	35. till
2. although	19. just once	36. unless
3. as	20. lest	37. until
4. as far as	21. now	38. when
5. as if	22. now since	39. whenever
6. as long as	23. now that	40. where
7. as soon as	24. now when	41. whereas
8. as though	25. once	42. where if
9. because	26. provided	43. wherever
10. before	27. provided that	44. whereas
11. even	28. rather than	45. whether
12. even if	29. since	46. which
13 ever though	30. so that	47. while
14. even when	31. supposing	48. who
15. if	32. than	49. whether or not
16. if only	33. that	50. whoever
17. if when	34. though	51. why

Types of Dependent Clauses:

1. Adverbial clause: When the games end, I will go home.

2. Adjective clause: The man who is wearing a black hat is happy. (IdentifyingMr. Bork, who works at the bank, lives on my street. (Non-identifying   – note the comma usage).

3. Noun Clause: I suggested that the world is flat. (Noun clause in the object position)
   When spoken I suggested the world is flat.
   ('That' is generally not spoken in conversation – or recordings.)

Compound-Complex Sentences:

A Compound-Complex must have at least two independent clauses and one dependent clause.
RULE

This type of sentence is critical to understand for Summarize Written Text as most answers m▪

be at least thirty words and usually involve a cause & effect essay summary. Having said that, to remember the longest sentence in the English language is presently at *13,955 words in Jonathan Coe's novel <u>The Rotter's Club</u>. The following are different forms of Compound complex sentences (note the different positions of the independent and dependent clauses):

1.   The men worked hard in the afternoon; it was a payday <u>where they were to receive their bonus for the year.</u> [IC; IC <u>DC</u>]

2.   <u>Although the women worked in the rain</u>, the work wasn't difficult; moreover, they could talk <u>while they worked</u>. [<u>DC</u>, IC; moreover, IC <u>DC</u>]

3.   Dogs often pant <u>when they are hot</u>, and this helps them cool down. [IC <u>DC</u>, IC]

4. Reading Skills

Reading Skills

The typically Reading Skills used at every secondary and tertiary school include Skimming, Scanning, Through Comprehension, and Critical Thinking. However, skimming on this test is only used if the test-takers 'looks over' the text to discover to discover its genre or field of interest. Likewise, there will no questions asking the test-taker to judge a situation critically. Therefore, the only skills needed will be scanning, looking for particular information, and through comprehension, which will involve several micro-skills.

Reading Skills to know:

Skimming:

- Skimming is quick reading for general ideas.
- When you skim you move your eyes quickly to acquire a basic understanding of the text.
- You do not need to read everything, and you do not need to read carefully.
- You read quickly the title and subtitles and topic sentences.
- You look at pictures charts and graphs.

Scanning:

How to scan

1. Decide exactly <u>what information</u> you are looking for <u>and what form</u> it is likely to take. For example, if you are looking for 'how much; something costs, you are looking for a number; if looking for 'who', you look for a person's name; if looking for when something starts, a time or a date etc.
2. <u>Decide where to look for the information</u>: for example, if looking up a name in a phone book, you look for the first letter of the person's surname; if looking for the Entertainment section in a newspaper, you look for that Section of the paper etc.
3. <u>Move you eyes quickly down the page until you find what you want</u>. Read to get the information.
4. When you find what you need, you usually stop reading.

Through Comprehension:

- When you read for Thorough Comprehension, you try to understand the total meaning of the reading.
- You want to know the details as well as the general meaning of each section.

If you have thoroughly comprehended a text, you have done the following:

- 1. Understood the main ideas and the author's point of view
- 2. Understood the relationships of ideas in the text, including how they relate to the author's purpose
- 3. Note that some ideas and points of view that were not mentioned were, however, implied by the author (drawing inferences)
- 4. Understand the concepts in the passage as well as the vocabulary. This may require you **to guess the meaning of unfamiliar words from 'context'** (or look them up in the dictionary)

You have to use context clues – the words and phrases the author is using to defend or show bias to one side of an issue. Here you will come across the author' purpose for writing.

It helps you interpret the information an author tells you, and it helps you question what is written – or not written!

Authorial Purpose: (helpful on Duolingo for Reading – (*Identify the Idea, Highlight the Answer, Title the Passage* for example*)*

There are only 3 purposes to any text from the author's point of view:

1. **To inform**: teach, explain, illustrate, clarify - the reader's goal is to learn the information (newspapers, journals)

2. **To persuade**: not just inform … use the information to make a **logical argument** – to persuade/convince or change another person's opinion – examples…

Aristotle (**logos**, pathos, ethos) (advertisements) [**fact as statistics, quotes form experts – found in textbooks, and personal experience**]

3. **To entertain**: the goal is to entertain – as a reader should pay attention literary devices … The primary purpose to entertain
To share thoughts - insights

Author's can be positive about a subject, or they can be negative about a subject , or they can be 'indifferent'– this becomes apparent in their 'tone' or the words they use to describe.

Purpose:	Point of View:	Tone:
To Inform (using facts)	?	Neutral/serious
To Persuade	strong and against!	Negative/angry
(a position in debate)	strong and for!	Positive/hopeful
To Entertain	(varies with outlook of society)	- tone will be related
		(i.e., happy, joyful)

Critical Thinking: (Not asked to use on Duolingo)

- When we read critically, we draw conclusions and make judgements about the reading.
- We ask questions such as, "What inferences can be drawn from this?" "Do I agree with this point of view?" We often do this when we read, but in some cases it is more important than others, as, for example, when author's give opinions about important issues or when trying to make an important decision.

For a more comprehensive look at Reading Skills, Barrett's Taxonomy of reading skills is widely recognized: You can view or download this file:

http://joebyrne.net/Curriculum/barrett.pdf

5. The Paragraph Form

Writing Skills

Parts of the Duolingo test that employ writing skills: (1) Read and Complete, (2) Write About the Photo, (3) Read, Then Write, and the (4) Writing Sample (Short Essay).

Listen and Type: This task on the exam is straightforward, just type the sentence that you hear. **The best way to approach** this task is to type as much as you can remember on the first recording, then listen again and complete the sentence. Finally, check the sentences for accuracy one last time by listening to the recording a third (3rd) time.

Complete the Sentences: This involves selecting the proper word to fill in a blank in a text by choosing a word in the drop-down menu on the right side of the screen. This is a vocabulary exercise, but it is related to a Paragraph, which is possibly the most important skill to know on this test. For Complete the Sentences the test-taker should have an awareness of a Topic sentence, Support sentences, Examples/ Detail, and a conclusion sentence because the Vocabulary may be related to the position the blank is in relative to the paragraph.

A Paragraph:

A paragraph is a group of sentences where every sentence is about the same topic. There are usually 4 parts to a paragraph: 1. Topic sentence, 2. Support Sentences, 3. Detail or examples, and 4. A concluding sentence. To ensure that a paragraph is consistently about one topic, all writers use a topic sentence to tell the reader what the paragraph is about.

i.   **Topic sentence**

A topic sentence consists of two parts: 1. The topic 2. A controlling idea

The topic tells the reader the subject of the paragraph and the underlined controlling idea informs the reader of the main idea of a paragraph.

Note: Writers use the term controlling idea in their topic sentence, but for readers, this is the main idea of the paragraph.

For example, here is a paragraph.

PARAGRAPH 1

Elephants use their trunk in many useful ways. First, their trunk is convenient at watering holes. Elephants can draw water up to their trunk and then release it into their mouths to have a drink. Second, an elephant can use its trunk to eat. Elephants usually break away branches from trees and shrubs with their trunk, and then they feed themselves by directing the food to their mouths. Finally, elephants use their trunks to smell. Elephants raise their trunks high in the air above their heads to smell for water, food, or predators. In these ways, an elephant's trunk helps them survive.

The underlined sentence in the box above is the topic sentence. It contains the topic (elephants) and the controlling idea (use their trunk in many useful ways). This topic sentence tells the reader that *this paragraph will only be about the useful ways that an elephant uses its trunk*.

Here is the same paragraph again where the topic sentence is found in the last sentence.

PARAGRAPH 2

Have you ever seen an elephant use its trunk? Their trunk is convenient at watering holes because they can draw water up to their trunk and then release it into their mouths to have a drink. Also, an elephant can use its trunk to eat. Elephants usually break away branches from trees and shrubs with their trunk, and then they feed themselves by directing the food to their mouths. Finally, elephants use their trunks to smell. Elephants raise their trunks high in the air above their heads to smell for water, food, or predators. Elephants use their trunk in many useful ways.

Although the narrator asks you, the reader, a question, 'have you ever seen an elephant use its trunk?', this is not the topic sentence! Rather, the writer has chosen to replace the concluding sentence with a topic sentence and begin with 'an interest generating question' followed with Detail and Support Sentences before informing you of the topic sentence at the very end.

ii.   Support Sentences

Support sentences are called support sentences because they *'support'* the controlling idea foun in the topic sentence. Academic paragraphs usually have at least 3 support sentences because a writer's work can be deemed 'weak' if it is not convincing enough, but 3 properly written support sentences are typically used to prove to readers that their controlling idea in the topic sentence has merit.

In PARAGRAPH 1 below there are 3 support sentences (underlined herein)

> Elephants use their trunk in many useful ways. First, their trunk is convenient at watering holes. Elephants can draw water up to their trunk and then release it into their mouths to have a drink. Second, an elephant can use its trunk to eat. Elephants usually break away branches from trees and shrubs, and then they feed themselves by directing the food to their mouths. Finally, elephants use their trunks to smell. Elephants raise their trunks high in the air above their heads to smell for water, food, or predators. In these ways, an elephant's trunk helps them survive.

Elephants use their trunk in many useful ways. First, their trunk is convenient at watering holes Elephants can draw water up to their trunk and then release it into their mouths to have a drink Second, an elephant can use its trunk to eat. Elephants usually break away branches from trees and shrubs, and then they feed themselves by directing the food to their mouths. Finally, elephants use their trunks to smell. Elephants raise their trunks high in the air above their heads to smell for water, food, or predators. In these ways, an elephant's trunk helps them survive.

Notice, too, that each support sentence reflects 'a useful way' or the controlling idea found in t topic sentence. Likewise, detail or examples are used to complete the support sentences.

iii.   Detail

Each support sentence is also '*supported*' by detail. Detail or examples are used to complete the elaboration on the subject which helps 'round out' the overall expression of the controlling idea. For example, below, the details that back up the support sentences are underlined.

> Elephants use their trunk in many useful ways. First, their trunk is convenient at watering holes. Elephants can draw water up to their trunk and then release it into their mouths to have a drink. Second, an elephant can use its trunk to eat. Elephants usually break away branches from trees and shrubs with their trunk, and then they feed themselves by directing the food to their mouths. Finally, elephants use their trunks to smell. Elephants raise their trunks high in the air above their heads to smell for water, food, or predators. In these ways, an elephant's trunk helps them survive.

You can now see how a proper paragraph is written – Details back up the Support Sentences, and the Support Sentences support the Controlling Idea.

Topic sentence = (Topic + controlling idea)

↓

Support Sentence = supports ↑ the controlling idea

↓

Detail supports = ↑ the Support Sentence

It is important that test-takers are able to separate 'fact' from 'opinion'. Below are the typical ways in which 'fact' is used to support Supporting Sentences. Opinions have to be sustained by 'Fact' or the opinion/argument loses its credibility. In other words, facts are the evidence needed to make an opinion valid, so 'facts' remain as 'truth' by themselves.

FACT as:

i.   **Empirical Evidence** is usually used in the form of statistics (i.e. 33% of the population, 1/3 of the people etc.).

ii.   **Quotations** are usually reported in the first person from the perspective of an expert in the field of the given subject/topic.

iii.   **Examples** are used as either: (1) anecdotal evidence or from personal experience – 'the man that I saw was wearing a mask' (2) from a common 'accepted or universal truths' – 'nobody is perfect'; 'people cannot fly'; 'car drivers have accidents'.

iv.   **<u>Concluding Sentence</u>**

The concluding sentence of a paragraph can (1) summarise the main points of the paragraph, or (2) it can be a rewrite of the topic sentence, or (3) it can contain a future-leaning sentence that offers a warning or continued fulfillment. You can use one (1) of these conclusion types to complete your Survey, as in the Email you will write an 'outcome', usually.

In the paragraph below, the 'signal words', 'transition words' or 'cohesive devices' are underlined. In the concluding sentence 'In these ways' is a prepositional phrase that signals to the reader a 'summary' of the 'usefulness of an elephant's trunk' and is followed by a future-leaning statement that this 'usefulness' helps the elephant <u>to survive</u> (as we assume it lives in the wildness). So, 'In these ways' refers to the 3 ways in which an elephant can use its trunk, which in turn illustrates to the reader how the elephant 'survives'. Likewise, 'First', 'Second', and 'Finally' all allow for consistent, easy to follow, organized reading, which helps your 'readability'

Elephants use their trunk in many useful ways. <u>First</u>, their trunk is convenient at watering holes. Elephants can draw water up to their trunk and then release it into their mouths to have a drink. <u>Second</u>, an elephant can use its trunk to eat. Elephants usually break away branches from trees and shrubs with their trunks, and then they feed themselves by directing the food to their mouths. <u>Finally</u>, elephants use their trunks to smell. Elephants raise their trunks high in the air above their heads to smell for water, food, or predators. <u>In these ways</u>, an elephant's trunk <u>helps them survive.</u>

Note: PARAGRAPH 1 and 2 above are basic paragraphs that use all the typical parts of a paragraph.

Practice and More Understanding

Common Types of Phrases

1. Verb + (adjective) + Noun

He <u>likes pizza</u>. (verb + Noun)

<u>Have a good time</u> on vacation. (verb + adjective + noun)

2. Phrasal Verbs (Verb + a Preposition)

Please <u>turn off</u> the lights.

Can you <u>pick up</u> Mark after school?

3. Verb + Adjective/ Adverb

The house is big. (verb + adjective)

He was sick yesterday. (verb + adjective)

She <u>sits</u> alone. (verb + adverb)

4. Prepositional Phrase

The book in <u>on the table</u>.

<u>On Monday</u>, she walked to work.

5. Adjective + Noun

It is a <u>big house</u>.

It is <u>green door</u>.

He is a <u>magnificent musician</u>.

5. Adverbial Phrase

He looked to see <u>where his ball went</u>.

I want to know <u>why in this place</u>.

I know <u>how to fly a plane</u>.

I could not park <u>anywhere near the place</u>.

<u>After the game</u>, I went home

7. Noun + Preposition + Noun

<u>A glass of water</u>, please

<u>A bag of cement</u>, please

<u>A lot of people</u> live in my apartment block.

Topic Sentences

A topic sentence usually tells the reader (or listener) two things.

1. The topic of conversation

2. The controlling idea

For the Duolingo exam it should be the first sentence of your speech or written paragraphs.

The Controlling Idea is often confused with the Main Idea.

Remember this:

When you are the **writer**, you write a **controlling idea** in your topic sentence.

When you **read**, you look for the **Main Idea**, and this is usually the first sentence of a paragraph but sometimes you have to piece together the Main Idea from different sentences in a paragraph.

Basically, they are the same thing, but it depends on the activity you are doing.

Main Idea/ Controlling Idea

1. Tells the writer's idea about the topic.

It should tell of all the ideas and information that is written in the paragraph

It should NOT step-outside or include other ideas or information that are not in the paragraph.

The main idea/controlling idea is usually the first sentence in a paragraph, but sometimes you ave to add information from another sentence to complete the main idea (the controlling idea ould be in the first sentence as you are the writer)

or example:

Sports stars in the United States make a lot of money. This is especially true for the most popular team sports, such as basketball, hockey, football, and baseball. The best players in hese sports get millions of dollars from their organizations and owners. They can make even more money through advertising with different companies. These companies will pay a lot of money to have these athletes wear their products.

---

he Main Idea/ Controlling idea is the first sentence in the paragraph:

orts stars in the United States make a lot of money.

gives the topic – **Sports Stars** and the main idea/controlling idea – **make a lot of money**

ll the other sentences in the paragraph tell about this one idea.

Listening Skills

nerally, there are 2 approaches to practicing your listening ability – *Top down & Bottom Up*

- **Top-down approaches** focus on developing the learner's ability to understand the whole message by bringing meaning to it through their **knowledge of the world (knowledge of the subject matter of the text or listening material) and the application of prediction, deduction and inference skills.**

- **Bottom-up approaches** take language as the starting-point and focus on vocabulary and grammatical items as a means of understanding a piece of discourse.

Duolingo listening tasks include *Listen and Select*, *Listen and Type*, & *Listen, Then Speak*. Therefore, 2 of these Tasks can be practiced as Top Down (Listen, Then Speak, Listen and Typ and 1 (Listen and Select) as Bottom Up Listening Skills.

Since the Duolingo examine has an almost unlimited resource to choose from (approximately 1 million words in the English language and an infinite selection of sentences), The best a test-taker can do is be familiar with 'typical' words and sentences used for communication that rang from easy to more difficult (Level 1 to Level 3).

For **Bottom Up** practice, Test takers can try at the level of sound a Phonemic Chart to become familiar with individual sounds of the Alphabet with examples:

https://www.englishclub.com/pronunciation/phonemic-chart-ia.php

(Also, use an online dictionary for pronunciation, Part of Speech and meaning, too)

https://www.merriam-webster.com/ (click on the icon to hear the word spoken)

(Click on the individual letter for sound, or the word below to her an individual word spoken with a particular phoneme)

A phoneme is the (=) smallest alphabetic representation that a listener can use to differentiate words.

* Phoneme practice is just individual sounds, so try to practice listening to longer 'segments' o utterances (longer sentences) of listening.

Top-down practice uses your own knowledge of the language to help you 'predict' or use educated guesses (inferences) to understand sentence meaning. To this end there are many plac online practice. Here are 2 that I like:

1. https://www.englishclub.com/listening/ - many different listening activities to try here.

2. https://www.esl-lab.com/ - many easy, intermediate, and difficult quizzes on this site. The easier choices are not as long. The different contexts or situations help test-takers to become 'familiar' with different words and phrase used in English.

3. For **Listen and Type** there is a video at mjgeducation.com (Duolingo BLOG) where you can practice typing individual sentences (on your own) and check the answers.

PART 2

Types of Duolingo Exam Questions

There are approximately 17 different test questions on the Duolingo exam. Here they are with helpful methods, examples, and approximate 'screen shot frames'.

1. Read and Complete

Read and Complete simply asks the test-taker to complete the words in a paragraph. Test-takers should familiarize themselves with Parts of Speech at first and then add vocabulary. Remember there are three levels to *Read and Complete*, so your first attempt might be easy and then the next attempt maybe more difficult – the vocabulary increases the difficulty – know your suffixes.

Praxis: You must type in letters to complete words in a given paragraph.

Time: 3 minutes

TIPS:

Read the passage before focusing, trying to spell each word.

Use 'context clues' or the 'topic' and your background schemata on the topic to help you make educated guess about what the word (s) may be.

For example: 3:00

2:55 (clock time on screen)

Type the missing letters to complete the text below

My holid _ _ in Cuba was very excit _ _ _ . T _ _ food was g _ _ _ as well ...etc
(You should be prepared to fill in from 10 to 15 words in this Task)

Answer: My holiday in Cuba was very exciting. The food was good as well

---

You must know: Parts of Speech (see Appendix)

The key to this Duolingo task is to study all Parts of Speech and know Articles (a, an, and 'the') because many of the smaller words will be prepositions, articles, pronouns, conjunctions, or even interjections that need an exclamation mark (!). The larger words will possibly include adverbs, some verbs, adjectives, and nouns.

*Remember: Level 2 and 3 will use more difficult forms of words – adding suffixes to create different word forms.

Example:

Man _ _ pe_ _ _ think that s _ _ is suit _ _ _ _ f _ _ this j _ _ .

Many people think that she is suitable for this job.

When you fill in the blanks, the context (what is being said) and the grammar has to be correct to get maximum points.

Also, the English language syntax is usually written and spoken in the form Subject + Verb + Object, so by knowing this a test-taker can take advantage of this. For example, and object pronoun has to be 'after' the verb:

I wor_ _ _ wi_ _ h _ _.

I worked with <u>him</u>. Not, I worked with <u>he</u>.

(Object pronoun - him)   (Subject pronoun - he)

Approach: Read through the text sentence by sentence. With each sentence fill in all the smaller words first and then complete the longer words in the same sentence and then move on. Practice *Read and Complete* in Part 3. Answers can be found in Part 4.

2. Read and Select

Asks you to recognize 'real' English words presented in three rows.

Praxis: Just select a 'real' word by clicking on it with your mouse's cursor.

Time: 1:00 minute.

TIPS:

Read carefully. Some words will read differently due do letter changes in spelling.

You will probably do 2 or 3 of these tasks, so don't be concerned if one question has more 'real words' than the next question.

For example:

 1:00

.52 (clock time on screen)

Select the real English words from the list

neglor	rocket √	spoof	lift	jargot
peeple	runny	alone	hacken	mamotte
alive √	readile	effeck	elevator	hostile

You must know: Parts of Speech and knowledge of Vocabulary

Note*: One of the major assumptions that drives this task is that people can recognize 'real' English words if they are well read. Try to read in many different genre.

Listen and Select

ike Read and Select above, a test-taker must *Listen and Select* to identify real English words.

raxis: Click on the audio icon 🔊 to listen to a spoken word then click on the word if it is a eal' English word.

ime: 1:30

IPS:

- Listen carefully. Some words will sound not real. As a rule, if it 'sounds real', it is probably a 'real' English word. Likewise, if you have never heard the word before, it probably is not a 'real' English word -

- Click on the speaker icon to replay words as many times as you like.

 1:30

r example:

16

🔊 WORD 1	🔊 WORD 2	🔊 WORD 3
🔊 WORD 4	🔊 WORD 5	🔊 WORD 6
🔊 WORD 7	🔊 WORD 8	🔊 WORD 9

NEXT

u must know: Parts of Speech and knowledge of Vocabulary. Try to listen to many different ms of audio recordings (news, podcasts etc.) and watch/listen to YouTube or movies.

4. **Listen and Type**

Just type what you hear. You will hear a spoken sentence. Then you must type the sentence **exactly** as it is spoken.

Praxis: Click on the icon to hear the recording and type in the box on the computer screen

Time: 1:00 minute.

TIP:

You can listen to the sentence 3 times in total, so it is best if you type what you heard after the listening and then check your typing by listening a second time and third time.

For example:

 1:00

Type the statement you hear

(type box)
The doctor will call you in the morning.

Number of replays left 1

NEXT

You must know: Practice using your short-term memory for sentences between 7 and 14 words in length. Some practice recording on the MJG Education website.

5. Read Aloud

Just 'Read' the statement presented on the page.

Praxis: You must click on a record button then read the sentence presented on the page.

Time: 20 seconds.

TIPS:

You only have 20 seconds, so if you have time, say the statement out loud 1 time before you record it.

This task is graded by an algorithm, so speak at an even tempo while reading. Try not to speed up and slow down.

For real time examples of how to read, go to the blog at mjgeducation.com (type in Duolingo for all results)

For example:

 :20

Record yourself saying the statement below

:05

 "The climate change problem is everybody's problem."

* Recording   ·ı|ı··ı·

NEXT

You must know: Speak clearly at an even pace.

Read Aloud is a straightforward exercise where the test-taker reads a sentence into a microphone. This task has three different levels that move from Level 1, short sentences or questions to Level 2, where the sentences or questions are a little longer, perhaps with noun clauses and a couple 3 syllable words, to Level 3, that includes longer sentences (compound sentences usually), more perfect verb tenses, and more multi-syllable words. The Passive Voice may be used as well, but you just have to read most sentences in a regular or normal manner – as if you are answering a question in a classroom or talking with a new friend.

For example:

Level 1

A. **Do you like my car?** (Note that this is a Yes or No question – your intonation (the rise and fall of your voice) should rise to the question mark (as with above question) or the end of the question. 'Do you like ↑ my ↑ car↑?

Yes or no questions always begin with a verb or a modal verb (Should, Could, Would, May be..etc.)

Good English speakers will also let their intonation fall with 'Wh' or information questions, such as 'What is your name↓?

Just be wary of the question form if it comes up on the *Read Aloud* task.

Many statements you will read will not have any intonation.

For example:

B. We do not have gym class today. (No intonation)

C. He likes to ride his bicycle. (No intonation)

Level 2

A. She sometimes works at the library on the weekends.

B. My girlfriend said she would wait at the bookstore for me.

C. She is certain that our instructor will give extra marks.

Level 3

A. I do not know what the movies is about or who the leading actors are.

B. She will have returned from Japan and started her new job when you have permission to relocate.

C. Cartological and azimuth readings are corrected, and the atmospheric tests are done as well.

6. **Write about the Photo**

Praxis: Look at a photograph and describe what you see.

Time: 1:00 minute.

TIPS:

In your first sentence describe or state the main object in the photo
Write more than one sentences if you have time.

For example:

You must know: Organized response: Topic sentence + detail (in the foreground, in the background).

 1:00

:45

Write one or more sentences that describe the image

This an image of a cow in a field. In the background I can see two or three other cows. The cow is standing on green grass.

NEXT

Example: **Write About the Photo**

The method for *Write about the Photo* is always the same – describe what you see. So, you must write a topic sentence first and add a sentence or two to get a high mark. The directions ask for 1 sentence, but you should try to write 2 or 3.

Method:

1. Describe what you see – generally.

2. Write a sentence about the foreground (Use the 'foreground' – in front of the subject(s))

3. Write a sentence about the background. (Use the word 'background' – behind the subject(s))

OR 4. Write about how you feel when you look at this picture.

For the picture above:

The image shows a woman and boy on a boat. In the foreground, I see the boy is sitting on the woman's lap. In the background, I can see 2 or 3 islands and the stirred-up water behind the boat

OR

The image shows a woman and boy on a boat. They look to be a mother and son as the boy is sitting in the mother's lap. They look happy on the water together.

Of course, you can write 1 sentence, but a second and/ third sentence written in the 1-minute given will help get you a higher score.

Please see many more examples in Part 3

Speak about the Photo

Praxis: Look at a photograph, click on the record button and describe what you see in words.

Time: 30 seconds to 1:30 maximum.

TIPS:

This task gives 20 seconds to look at the photo before recording begins.

Use this time to organize your response.

This task is graded by an algorithm, so try to speak at an even pace and begin with a proper topic sentence and then give Support, detail/ example sentences, and a conclusion if you have time (i.e., Paragraph form)

For example:

:30 to 1:30

Record yourself saying the statement below

45

* Recording

NEXT

You must know: Organized response: Topic sentence + detail (in the foreground, in the background). Try to be descriptive using accurate adjectives and nouns.

Speak about a Photo

The pictures in this task seemingly increase in complexity as they provide more items to talk about in the 30 to 90 seconds you have to speak. These questions and pictures are considered 'open response', but if you provide an organized response your score will increase dramatically as opposed to just speaking about a picture in any way you choose.

1. While speaking from 30 to 90 seconds, choose 3 things in the image to discuss.

2. Be aware you have to move around in this picture 'spatially', so use the terms: In the foreground, I can see ....; In the background, I can see...; In the middle area, I can see. Use these terms and describe what you see somewhat accurately and you will be guaranteed a 7 higher score because you are organized – spatially – and the algorithm will 'recognize' these movements with language!

3. Also, use prepositions of place, next to, beside, on top of, between, etc.

4. Use adjectives to give color or to describe.

Method:

While speaking for 30 to 90 seconds, use a paragraph form and spatial prepositional phrases.

1. **Topic sentence** = a general overview of the picture
2. **In the foreground**, I can see … (next to, beside, in front of, between, etc. (a noun)
3. **In the background**, I can see …(next to, beside, in front of, between, etc. (a noun)
4. **In the middle area**, I can see …(next to, beside, in front of, between, etc. (a noun)
5. **A conclusory statement**: (i.e., There is a lot going on in this picture.)

For example: Level 1 photo

> This is a picture of three women standing together on a beach. An older woman is in between two younger women, perhaps her daughters, and all three are looking towards a camera. In the background, I can see ocean tide running onto the beach. It must be cold as all three women are wearing sweaters.

Please see more examples for Level 2 and 3 in Part 3

3. **Read, Then Write**

Praxis: Answer a question given on the screen in writing.

Note: The answer will disappear after 30 seconds, so you have to remember it as you continue to write. A proper topic sentence will help you remember the question prompt.

Time: 5:00 minutes.

TIPS:

Write a paragraph using proper paragraph form (strive for 100+ words).

Reread your paragraph for errors if you have time before going on to the next question.

For example:

5:00

Respond to the Question in at least 50 words

	Your response here:
Describe a time when you were responsible to complete a task.	

NEXT

You must know: Paragraph form. You can make up a response if necessary as you are being marked on your writing ability!

Read, the Write gives test-takers 5-minutes to write a complete paragraph. * Remember, you can make up a story or an event to complete this task.

Paragraph form:

Topic Sentence – topic and controlling idea.

Support Sentence 1

Detail/ example sentence

Support Sentence 2

5

Detail/ example sentence

Support Sentence 3

Detail/ example sentence

Concluding Sentence

- Note: there are 8 sentences in the paragraph form above to write. If a test-taker averages 13 to 20 words a sentence, he or she will easily write over 100 words.

For example: **Describe a time you were surprised. What happened?**

I was surprised when I won a free trip to Florida. I bought a ticket for a prize draw at our local mall. The grand prize was a new car, but I won the second-place prize. I had completely forgotten about the ticket I bought because the draw was 2 months after I bought the ticket. However, I did think about winning a new car. I imagined myself driving around the city 'looking good'. In any event, my husband received the phone call that we won a trip to Florida. We were happy with that because we could take a vacation, and we were both surprised because we never really won anything! (112 words)

Topic Sentence: I was surprised when I won a free trip to Florida.

Support Sentence 1: I bought a ticket for a prize draw at our local mall.

Detail/ example sentence: The grand prize was a new car, but I won the second-place prize.

Support Sentence 2: I had completely forgotten about the ticket I bought <u>because the draw was 2 months after I bought the ticket.</u>

Detail/ example sentence: <u>because</u> the draw was 2 months after I bought the ticket. (Complex sentence)

Support Sentence 3: However, I did think about winning a new car.

Detail/ example sentence: I imagined myself driving around the city 'looking good'.

Concluding Sentence(s): In any event, my husband received the phone call that we won a trip to Florida. We were happy with that because we could take a vacation, and we were both surprised because we had never really won anything!

*Remember: As long as your response is organized and attempts to vary Sentence Structure, you will score high on this task. The algorithm that reviews your writing searches for organization structures in your writing:

Note the signal words: 'However' and 'In any event'

The Topic sentence is most important because it answers, 'Did the test-taker answer the question?' Then a series of Support and detail/ examples sentences show you are giving an organized response. A concluding sentence(s)(maximum of 2 sentences) that refers back to the topic sentence, summaries your paragraph, or offers a future outcome completes a perfect response.

Please see many more examples in the Part 3

9. **Read, Then Speak**

Praxis: Read a question and its subsections then click on the record button to answer.

Time: 30 seconds to 1:30 minute maximum.

TIPS:

This task is marked by an algorithm, so speak at an even pace and answer all of the questions. Use a topic sentence to begin and then answer the sub-questions and give detail/examples to each.

For example:

0:30 minimum

1:30 maximum

Prepare to speak for at least 30 seconds about the question below

Describe your favorite sport to watch on T.V.

- What is it?
- Why do you like it?
- When do you watch it?
- Why is it your favorite sport?

Record Now

ou must know: Paragraphing – Topic sentence –'organized response' with Support sentences
d examples/ detail. Try to speak at an even pace, not too fast or not too slow.

ad, then Speak is a task that asks the test-taker to respond in 30 to 90 seconds about a series of
estions to be read on the page before them. The first thing to be read is the General Statement
fore a series of questions. The questions are simple 'conversation points' that allow you to
tend your answer past the 30 second minimum limit.

- Remember, as it says in the Duolingo guide, " just like with writing, vary your
  sentence structure and word choice as much as possible."

is means that you should give an organized response when you speak as well! So, start with a
ic sentence and allow the 'questions to be the support sentences' and then add examples. If
u have time, add a concluding sentence.

example, from the Duolingo website:

lk about a hobby or activity that you enjoy doing?

- **What is it?**
- **How long have you been doing it?**

55

- **Who do you do it with?**
- **Why is it important to you?**

My favorite hobby is Reading. I have been reading all sorts of books for 15 years. Because I study Economics at college now, I tend to read more business journals and articles. It is a lonely task, but sometimes I can discuss what I read with friends or my classmates. Reading is important because I read fiction and non-fictitious books and it increases my understanding on many topics and vocabulary. These things will be important when I graduate and deal with clients after I land my first job. (88 words)

Please see more examples in Part 3

10. Listen, Then Speak

Praxis: Click on the listening icon ◀)) to hear a question. Then click on the recording button

 to record your answer to the question.

Time: 30 seconds to 1:30 minute maximum.

TIPS:

You can replay the listening prompt as many as 3 times before the recording starts.

When the 'Next' button turns orange, you can start your recording.

This task is graded by an algorithm, so try to speak at an even pace and begin with a proper top sentence and then give Support, detail/ example sentences and a conclusion if you have time (i.e., Paragraph form)

For example:

0:30 Minimum

1:30 Maximum

1:04

Speak the answer to the question you hear

Number of replays left 2   (maximum 3)

· · | | | · · · ·

* Recording

| NEXT |

You must know: Topic sentence – organized response with Support sentences and examples/ detail.

This task asks the test-taker to listen to question/prompt (statement) and then record an answer. You can listen to the question/prompt 3 times in 20 seconds, and then you have between 30 and 90 seconds to respond.

You will have to answer to a statement (A) or a question prompt (B)

Statement – A: Describe your favorite movie.

Question – B: What do you think about global warming these days?

Prompt = Statement or Question

In any event, just like Read, Then Speak above, you should give an organized response where you give support statements and examples/detail and, time permitting, a concluding sentence

Topic sentence = topic + controlling idea

A: **Describe your favorite movie**

'My favourite movie is Hunt for Red October. I enjoy this movie because it involves submarine warfare, and it includes one of my favorite actors, Sean Connery. Although Sean Connery has passed away, he was one of the first James Bond's acters, so he has had a lot of experience in 'lead roles'. In Hunt for Red October he is the commander of a Russian submarine who intend to defect to the United States of America. There are many 'cool' underwater battle scenes, and there are great depictions of military protocol. This is why this is my favorite movie.' (99 words)

B: **What do you think about global warming these days?**

Well, I think global warming will be an ongoing problem for several reasons. First, there are too many cars and airplane flights in the world, and they all pollute the air and add to warming the earth. Second, governments around the world are not doing enough, even though the head of the United Nations stated the world is trouble due to climate change. Finally, there is not enough research done for effective alternative energy resources. Research requires financing and no country wants to take the lead. In conclusion, these are the reasons I think global warming will continue to be a problem. (102 spoken words)

Please see more examples for Listen, Then Speak in the **Practice Section**

11. **Complete the Sentences**

This test item is better known as a 'Fill in the Blank' exercise. A test-taker has to choose words from the right side of the page to 'fill in' blank areas in a sentence. Usually, this exercise is presented in the form of a paragraph with several sentences that have blanks. There may be up to 5 blanks to fill in and you may have to do up to 6 of these exercises in the time allotted– it depends when the algorithm or grading engine is 'satisfied'.

Praxis: Click your cursor on the word you have chosen to fill in the gap in a sentence from the right side of the computer page.

Time: 7:00 or 8 minutes.

TIPS:

Read the entire passage first then read an individual sentence and from the 'context' – the topic and your background knowledge (schemata), make an educated guess as to which word is correct to complete the sentence.

You can fill in the words in in the paragraph in any order (i.e., fill in the 4th blank if it is the most obvious for you, then do the 2nd blank – the order you fill in the blanks does not matter, but to finish as many paragraphs as the exam offers (3 – 6 paragraphs in 7-8 minutes).

For example:

7 or 8 minutes

6:44

Quit Test

Passage	Select the best option for each missing word
Not all of the Hawaiian Islands are popular tourist spots. In fact, one of them is (1)_____ and (2) _____ to tourists. That is the island of Kahoolawe, the smallest of the Hawaiian Islands. Many years ago, this island was covered with vegetation: today it is (3)_____ and (4)_____. Nevertheless, businessmen flock to the area seeking ways to (5) _____ this island.	1. Drop-down choices 2. Drop-down choices 3. Drop-down choices 4. Drop-down choices 5 Drop-down choices

Next

You must know: Vocabulary, Paraphrase, Paragraphing with Support sentences and examples/ detail.

Essentially, this task asks the test-taker to fill in the blanks in a paragraph with a word from a drop-down menu to the far right of the page. There are several things to be wary of on this task.

Procedure

1. ALWAYS READ TO THE END OF THE CLAUSE OR SENTENCE; NEVER STOP AT THE BLANK AND CHOOSE! You need the full context of the sentence to answer correctly, but many people incorrectly stop at the blank and choose.

2. Check: after you choose a word, read the sentence to see if it is grammatically correct – some words are decoys that 'sound' okay, but are not the correct 'form' of word.

3. Know your parts of speech (i.e. do not place a noun in front of another noun when an adjective is needed. This is sometimes the easiest way to place a word because only one of the choices is 'an adjective' let's say! Try to recognize the part of speech of each word offered.

4. Know your syntax (i.e. statements usually run Subject + Verb + Object).

'**Me** go home' is not correct in terms of syntax because and object pronoun (Me) is used after the verb not before it as a Subject. 'Mark, **give me** the book.' This is common sense, but pronouns sometimes get confused.

5. Choose the correct word to fill the blank.

5. Paragraphing (i.e., the paragraph given will have a topic sentence, so try to recognize it. This can help choose the correct word by context)

For example: *This is a similar exercise below, but without the dropdown boxes to the right.

Click on the appropriate number to the right of the page to access the drop-down list of choices. Select the appropriate answer choice for each blank.

Researchers have engineered a low-cost plastic material that could become the basis for clothing that cools the wearer, reducing the need for _____ 1. **energy-consuming / energy-engrossing / energy-absorbing / energy-devouring** air conditioning. Describing their

---

work in Science, the researchers suggest that this new family of fabrics could become the basis for 2. **costumes/garments/outfits/attires** _____ that keep people cool in hot climates without air conditioning. "If you can cool the person rather than the building where they work or live, that will save energy," said Yu Xiao, an associate professor at Stanford. This new material works by allowing the body to 3. **remove / discharge / dismiss / eject** _____ heat in two ways that would make the wearer feel nearly 4 degrees Fahrenheit cooler than if they wore cotton clothing. The material cools by letting perspiration 4. _____ **evaporate/vaporize/volatilize/condense** through the material, something ordinary fabrics already do. But the Stanford material provides a second, revolutionary cooling mechanism: allowing heat that the body emits as infrared radiation to pass through the plastic textile.

ate, T. (2016, September 1). *Engineers develop a plastic clothing material that cools the skin*. Retrieved January , 2023, from https://www.sciencedaily.com/releases/2016/09/160901151933.htm

the example above, the background schemata refer to engineering, perhaps chemical engineering, and there is an explicit reference to 'Science' magazine (real world) Notice, too, at all the options at **1.** have 'ing' or present participle/gerund endings. Here energy-engrossing and energy-devouring can be eliminated immediately because the former does not answer the context (reducing); rather, it means 'to get your attention', and the latter is an opinion as a personification (to give human qualities to an inanimate object). The final two, energy-absorbing and energy-consuming, are close in meaning, but by way of collocation, energy-absorbing becomes the correct answer (words that are used more frequently in a particular order than others with similar meanings). Of course, test-takers are well read to notice collocations.

2., three of the four choices have a specific purpose (attire, costumes, outfits) where only 'garments' remains neutral to fit the context of a 'new family of fabrics'.

only one word can fit the blank precisely.

3., eject and dismiss are immediately eliminated as the body does not eject; unless it is a crude deduction referring to a type of sickness or as another personification, nor dismiss because the body does not order itself to do anything! Therefore, the better choice between remove and discharge is 'discharge' because this the scientific term commonly used to describe the process of transferring heat into the atmosphere, whereas 'remove' contains the context of 'lifting' something and then removing it.

Scientific words over a slightly more inappropriate word

At **4.**, perspiration is closer to water than a chemical that 'vaporizes' or 'volatilize'(s) at room temperature. Thus, both words can be eliminated on the basis of context – yes, perspiration can be argued to be a chemical reaction and react, in certain circumstances, not unlike a vapor or volatilize, but you have to use common sense as well. We have all sweat/perspire and the cooling feeling we feel on our skin is not of a hastened chemical reaction. On the contrary, this is why condense is eliminated because we feel warmer when perspiration is 'wet' on our skin. The correct response is 'evaporate' as it is akin to the water cycle.

Common sense

NOTE: With *Complete the Sentences*, there are 2 areas of inquiry that are part of the machinations you must go through to get the correct answer:

1. The precise meanings of the words

2. The context that the words are used in

Note*: Read through the entire passage before attempting to fill in the blanks.

Please see more examples for *Complete the Sentences* in the **Part 3**

12. Complete the Passage

This is another form of a fill in the blank exercise whereby the test-taker has to complete a paragraph with the appropriate sentence instead of a single word.

Praxis: Choose the sentence on the right side of the page to fill in a gap between two sentence There may be <u>6 of these tasks</u> to complete in the 7 to 8 minutes. Again, it depends on when the algorithm is 'satisfied'.

Time: 7 or 8:00 minutes.

TIPS:

Read each passage on both sides of the gap and try to understand the context – find the topic sentence!

The sentence that completes the paragraph will undoubtedly be a Support or detail/example! For example:

 7 or 8minuites

6:31

Quit Test

Passage French and English doctors sometimes have different ideas about medical care. In France, doctors often give strong medicine to move blood to the brain. However, doctors in England do not think that is helpful.	Select the best sentence to fill in the blank 1. French doctors worry too much. 2. French doctors are just like English doctors. 3. French doctors often worry about a patient's liver and diet. But English doctors do not. And French doctors take stomach illnesses very seriously.
But in England, doctors often say that stomach problems are not serious at all. They usually think stomach problems are caused by worrying too much. French Doctors are usually interested in trying out a variety of new treatments. English doctors, however, first wait to see if the new treatments really work.	4. French doctors stand in the doorways and thing about English doctors. 5 French doctors consider the opinions of the patient and then consult an English doctor as to what the best medicine is.

Next

You must know: Reading, Paragraphing- especially with Support Sentences and examples/ detail.

This task is basically about how well a test-taker understands the Paragraph form. Because the test-taker has to choose a sentence or two to '*Complete the Passage*', he or she should be aware that 98% of the time the choice will be either a Support Sentence (supporting idea, the main idea, or controlling idea), or an example that illustrates a Supporting Sentence, or both – usually a 2 sentence maximum length for this exercise. Test-takers should be able to score 100 % on this exercise if they can locate the topic sentence of the paragraph and read forward in the text to know what should come next or is missing from the text.

Procedure:

1. Read the 1st half of the text and try to fully understand the topic sentence (Topic + Controlling idea/ Main idea) so that you know what the paragraph is about.

2. Just read through the options to the right

3. Read the second 2nd half of the text

4. Know a paragraph outline (since you are undoubtedly looking for a Support Sentence or an example (or both) to complete this passage

5. Choose the correct sentence from the right side of the page.

For example:

A sub-species of grizzly bear has been discovered in Canada's Yukon quite by accident. Biologist Alan Parsons and his partner Elaine Bennis were gathering fern spores for lab analysis when they came across an abandoned bear cub.	**Select the best sentence to fill in the blank in the passage**: i. The bear cub was lost in the forest. ii. The bear cub made hand signals to the humans to show it was in trouble.
After nursing the cub for five days, the pair returned with the cub to Vancouver, where they delivered it to the city's South Park Zoo. It was at this point that that the Zoo's on-call mammologist and bear specialist, Dr Tim Whatley, made the discovery of the Ursidae sub-species.	iii. It was breathing shallowly and appeared close to death, so the scientists took it back to their research camp. iv. The bear no attempt to open its eyes when poked with a stick.

Please see more examples for *Complete the Passage* in Part 3

13. **Highlight the Answer**

Praxis: Read a question on the page. Then read the passage (a paragraph) on the page. Then Highlight the correct answer by dragging the part of the text that answers the question. Your answer will show in the box at the bottom of the page, so you can check your answer. Click the next button to continue to the next question and text. You may do this task up to 6 times in the time allotted.

Time: 7:00 or 8 minutes for up to 4 of the same type questions.

TIPS:

Highlight only the answer to the question asked. This may only be a word, a phrase, or an entire sentence.

Read your highlighted text and check 'your answer' before you go to the 'next' question. Try to be precise with your answers as you will do 6 of these questions in the allotted time. For example:

 7 or 8minuites

4:22

| Quit Test |

Passage	Click and drag text to highlight the answer below.
The ocean floor is an area almost 2.5 times greater than the total land area of the planet. Researchers are able to see where tectonic plates had slipped and slid over the millennia. In an ongoing process, convection currents in the molten mantle cause the plates to slowly move about the Earth at a rate of a few centimetres each year. Many ocean floor features are a result of the interactions that occur at the edges of these plates. Shifting plates may converge, diverge or transform each other. As plates converge, one plate may dive under the other causing earthquakes, forming volcanoes, or creating deep ocean trenches. Where plates have diverged from each other, molten magma has flowed upward between the plates forming mid-ocean ridges, underwater volcanoes, hydrothermal vents, and new ocean floor crust. The Mid-Atlantic Ridge is an example of this type of plate boundary. Boundaries known as 'transform boundaries' are formed when two plates slide past one another. This is seen in mid-ocean ridges which are often associated with earthquakes due to zig-zag offsets.	How do undersea earthquakes occur? 'Highlight text in the passage to set the answer' Next

You must know: Reading: Scanning technique, Paragraphing

This task asks the test-taker to 'Highlight' (copy by dragging the mouse's cursor) the part of the text that answers a question. This is scanning!

Procedure:

1. Read the question first.

Then read the entire passage or 'Scan' for the answer to the question

Highlight the answer (just the answer or the entire sentence where the answer is found)

NOTE – never copy more than one sentence of the text as your answer will be considered wrong. If you are confronted with a sentence that has several clauses (compound complex), only highlight the clause with the answer!

For example:

France was ruled by monarchs for a period of 1362 years up until 1848. Though most died of illness or old age, many suffered at the hands of their countrymen. Louis XVI for example, lost his throne during the French Revolution of 1789 and was eventually guillotined in 1793. His wife, Marie Antoinette, was executed later the same year. Several French monarchs were assassinated or poisoned. After the July Revolution of 1830 the then reigning king, Charles X, fled France with his life under threat. He was succeeded to the crown by Louis-Philippe d'Orleans, who several years later, fearing for his life, fled to England booking passage under the pseudonym, Mr. Smith. Louis-Philippe, or Mr. Smith, was the last of the French monarchs.

Click and drag text to highlight the answer to the question below:

What is the original name of France's last King?

You would highlight the whole sentence or just the part of the sentence that contains the answer:

He was succeeded to the crown by Louis-Philippe d' Orleans

Louis-Philippe d' Orleans

Please see more examples for *Highlight the Answer* in the **Part 3**

14. Identify the Idea

Praxis: Click on the Idea on the right side of the page that best expresses the **main idea** of the passage (paragraph) you read on the left.

Time: 7:00 or 8 minutes for a maximum of 6 questions or until the algorithm is satisfied.

TIPS:

Read all answer options -don't choose quickly.

The idea that is correct will resemble a topic sentence. The Main idea can be pieced together from 'context clues' throughout the passage. The correct answer should be apparent after a clos reading of the text.

For example:

 7 or 8 minutes for possibly six 'Identify the Idea' passages.

2:14

Quit Test

For example:

Select the idea that is expressed in the passage:

Prizes and certificates are awarded, and many people give speeches. Very often a community leader or well-known politician gives a speech. It is common for the best students in the graduating class to give speeches to their classmates and families. These speeches focus on the accomplishments of the past and hopes for the future. Everyone feels good, and the event is a celebration of	Identify the idea in the passage from the following choices: (usually found to the far right of the page on the exam)
	a. This event is about speeches an families.
	b. This event is about student frustration and happiness.
	c. This event is a graduation ceremony.

the work that the students have completed during four years of high school. Some students will go to college. Others will begin working, or get married, or join the army. No one wants to think about problems they have or may have in the future	d. This even represents the typical choices made by students.

You must know: Reading for Topic Sentence or Main Idea (usually repeats the idea through Paraphrases), Paragraphing.

This task asks the test-taker to find the MAIN IDEA of a paragraph. To do exceedingly well on this task try to find the Topic sentence because the 'Main Idea' is also the 'controlling idea' when you write a paragraph – they are the same. As with the paragraph below, there is 'No' topic sentence, so the test-taker must make inferences, or educated guesses as to what the paragraph is about. Usually, synonyms are used for the same idea several times in a paragraph, so it should be easy to locate.

Procedure:

1. Read the passage one time and note the 'synonymous repetition of words or phrases'

2. Try to locate a Topic sentence – if none, ask yourself what is repeated most often

3. Read the 4 possible answers carefully

4. Try to Read only the Support sentences and/ the repeated parts in the paragraph and then compare with the answers

5. Try to write your own topic sentence in your mind – this will be close to one of the answers given

. The answer choices may try to offer detail or examples, never choose these – the answer should read like a topic sentence – not being too SPECIFIC like detail or an example.

15. **Title the Passage**

Praxis: Choose a suitable topic from the passage you read. There will 4 choices to choose from.

Time: 7:00 or 8 minutes for all 6 questions unless the algorithm is 'satisfied' with fewer responses.

TIPS:

Read all of the options – don't choose quickly.

Choose the title that has the topic and 'generally' covers all areas mentioned in the text.

For example:

 7 or 8 minutes for all six

questions

5:14

Quit Test

Passage	Select the best title for the passage.
We think of sleep as a time when the mind and body shut down. But this is not the case; sleep is an active period in which a lot of important processes occur. How this happens and why our bodies need such a long period of inactivity is still a mystery. But scientists understand some of sleep's functions, and the reasons we need it for better health and wellbeing.	1. How much sleep do we need? 2. What is a good night's sleep? 3. The importance of sleep for young people 4. Why do we need sleep?
	Next

You must know: Reading for Topic Sentence or Main Idea, Paragraphing

This Task asks the test-taker to 'Select the best title of the passage'. The best way to do so is by know what a Title phrase always has:

1. Titles always indicate accurately the subject and scope of the study.
2. Titles avoid using abbreviations.
3. Titles use words that create a positive impression and stimulate reader interest.
4. Titles use current words and idea from a particular field of study.

Procedure:

1. Read the passage – find the Topic Sentence (the topic or what the text/paragraph is about should be obvious)

*Note: The title is a "privileged" place in the text, because it draws the reader's most complete attention – it must draw your interest and be accurate

2. How is the audience for this text? Sometimes, titles are easy to choose, or eliminate choices, because a text may be written for 'children' let's say, and not 'adults'.

3. Read the passage again and then read the 'Title' options.

4. Choose the title that most accurate reflects what you have just read.

It might be a catchy phrase and not serious in tone - *It's a Frog's Life.* This title generalizes the passage.

Or it may be serious and more academic: *A Description of the Habitat, Lifespan and Breeding Patterns of the South American Tree Frog.* This title 'summarizes' the entire passage.

Since the text you will read is only a paragraph or 2 in length, you should be able to winnow down an answer quickly and accurately. Your choice has to be accurate to the passage whether all the 'Title choices' are general or summarized, so read the title choices carefully.

For example

Select the best title of the passage.

Our small city is characterized by a helpful way of life, a humble nature and spirit among residents. People who are familiar with our area and its snowy categorization are straightaway fascinated by the region's loveliness, legacy, moderate climate and hospitable sense.

A. Rodville, a Charming Way of Life.

B. Rodville, a Snowy Place in the Hills

C. Rodville, a Charming Place to Live.

D. Rodville, A Fun Place to Live.

Remember: A title's 'CONTENT words' are usually Capitalized, but the articles and prepositions are not (as seen in the example above).

16. **Writing Sample**

Praxis: You will be asked to write about a topic below for a maximum of 5 minutes. Write a short essay. You will have 30 seconds to organize your ideas before the recording begins.

This task is NOT marked, but it is sent to your prospective college, university, or employer.

Time: 3 to 5:00 minutes.

TIPS:

Use the essay form to organize your response – a 3 or 4 paragraph essay.
Vary your sentence structure and use 3 or 4 less common words (see Part 6)

For example:

 3 to 5 minutes for all six

questions

	Your response
Write for 3 to 5minutes about the topic below: Agree or disagree with this statement: "Electric vehicles are critical for the future of the earth" Explain your reasoning.	
	Next

You must know: Essay form, Paragraphing– Topic Sentence then (support and examples/detail), express 2 sides of an argument – 4 paragraph essay form.

For this task the test-taker must write consecutive paragraphs that mention **both sides of an argument.** This is typically a 4-paragraph response that includes:

Introduction

Body Paragraph (one side)

Body Paragraph (the other side)

A Conclusion Paragraph

Since this essay is to be written in a maximum of 5 minutes, the test-taker does not have to write lengthy essay. What is MOST IMPORTANT is that your response is organized!

For example: Question Prompt: Agree or Disagree with this statement:

New Technologies improve lives." Explain your reasoning.

NOTE: It does not matter what side of the argument you choose – you are being marked on the form of your response' by an algorithm, so there is no right or wrong answer. Just make sure

73

you choose a side of the argument where you can develop or give good reason(s) 'why' technology improves or makes life worse for people.

Essay 1:

Introduction

Some people argue that 'new technology' helps improve people's lives. Whereas others believe it does not. This essay will argue the former by way of explicit examples.

Body Paragraph 1:

There are many devices nowadays that improve people's lives for the better. The cellphone is a perfect example. A cellphone allows people to use email, access different applications, search the internet, or make a telephone call from most remote places throughout any city on a continent. This access to information has allowed the world to communicate at a greater rate than at any time in the past.

Body Paragraph 2:

Another device that improves lives is a Magnetic Resonance Image machine or MRI. In the medical field, this machine allows doctors to see all of a person's tissue in a particular area of the body. For example, MRI machines can illuminate blockages, torn ligaments, or broken bones immediately, so people can start to recover from their issues quicker. In this way, the MRI machine helps save people from a lot of pain and maybe even their life.

Conclusion (Summary)

In conclusion, both the Cellphone and MRI machine are examples of how 'newer technology' makes people's lives better. Cellphones make life easier by way of communication, and the MRI machine helps discover medical issues quicker, so people can recover quicker.

(212 words – approximately 42 words a minute)

NOTE*: This may be too long a response for some people to type in 5 minutes. Please see the next example below for a 3-paragraph response that is organized.

Essay 2:

Introduction

Although some people maintain 'new technology' has improved life on the planet, I tend to disagree with this statement.

Body Paragraph

How have computers, and by extension cellphones, made life better for people? These devices have allowed people to communicate quicker but at such a cost that people, ironically, do not communicate at all, really. Text messages and emails are all very fine, but it has come to the point where people do not sit face-to-face and talk anymore. For this reason, people do not even 'know' other people anymore. Also, both devices distract people from what they should be doing. It is far too easy to not do important work because people divert their attention too often to things that do not matter, like watching YouTube, playing a game on an app, or looking at pictures of celebrities!

Conclusion

In conclusion, with all the excitement around 'new technology' these days, it looks as if the future will lead people to become slaves to their devices and miss all the fun of real relationships with people face-to-face.

174 words – approximately 35 words a minute)

Note: 150-word organized responses should be a test-takers goal (approximately 30 words a minute)

Please see more examples in Part 3

7. Speaking Sample

Praxis: Test-takers will be asked to speak for 3 minutes upon a given topic written upon their computer screen. Directions will appear for 30 seconds (then disappear) before the recording starts. Your response will be recorded on Video.

Time: 1:00 to 3:00 minutes.

TIPS:

Give an organized response. Use a topic sentence to open and then Support, detail/example sentences, and a conclusion.

This task is NOT marked but it goes to the prospective college, university, or employer. Try to keep talking about relevant ideas related to your topic (paragraph form) and conclude after the 2-minute mark.

As this is a Video recording as well, **try to use your hands at times for emphasis** when you speak.

For example:

1:00 Minimum

3:00 Maximum

1:57

Speak for 1 to 3 minutes about the topic below

Who has had the most dramatic effect upon your life?

What effect(s) has this person had on your life?

* Recording

Record & Submit

You must know: Paragraphing – Topic Sentence then (support and examples/detail)

With this task you must Speak for 1 to 3 minutes, which is a very long time when speaking – so please practice with this time limit before you take the Duolingo exam. This task is really an extended version of Read, Then Speak because they usually ask a question and follow it with sub-questions. The directions will appear 30 seconds before the recording begins -so you should try to organize your response - unfortunately "no outside resources are allowed" which includes taking notes on paper or a cell phone (see Rules Section), so you have to stay organized in your mind. You have to try and remember the topic and the sub-questions in your head. THIS IS WHY PRACTICE IS SO IMPORTANT; practice answering everything with an organized response.

Note*: While the video is running for this response, remember that when the submit button 'turns orange' you have spoken for over 1 minute. Hopefully you can speak for over 2 minutes, speaking in a complete sentences – varying sentence structure and using contextual vocabulary.

For example:

Tell about your last vacation.

What is the importance of travel?

What do you think are the most popular holiday destinations?

Tips:

1. Use chronological order

2. Give reason (3 is best for maximum score)

3. Give 'benefits' and 'determents' (the pros & cons) if asked about a particular issue (global warming, taxes, employment etc.)

4. If all else fails – Speak out loud about the topic on what ever you think of (But stay on topic)

5. Use filler expressions, such as

'I have never thought about that before….'

'Uhm, let me see…..'

'I am not really sure what you mean…..on the one hand, do you mean..'

'Sorry, I just need a moment to think….'

'As I mentioned earlier….'

'One thing I forgot to mention…'

Generally, try to stay on topic at all times; however, when you shift the controlling idea, pause and speak, changing to another topic sentence (same topic but a different idea). You are being recorded on Video and this sometimes makes people extra nervous, but try to speak directly into the camera expressing your thoughts on different issues that surround the topic. Between 2 and 3 minutes should be your goal for the speaking sample.

More examples are found in Part 3

Part 3

Practice All Duolingo Tasks (<u>Answers follow in Part 4</u>)

Writing Tasks:

) Read and Complete

Level 1

Martin Luther King Jr. le_ man_ demonstrations against racism. H_ deliver__ his mess___

n a non-violent manner. So__ members of h__ movement later engag__ in less peace___

protests. Luther King w__ detained sever__ time_.

level 2

Many paren__ believe th__ sugar consump____ caus__ hyperactivity in th___ child___.

Indeed, 'sugar highs' are oft__ blam__ for rowdy___ or excitabil___. B__ is sug__ the

guilty par__, or is it simp__ a case of 'norm__' childh___behaviour?

level 3

Despite t__ fact that piranhas a__ relative__ harmless, many peop__ continue to believe t__

ervas___ myth that piranhas are danger___ to humans. Th__ impress___ of piranhas is

exacerbate__ by their mischaracteriza____ in popular med__. For example, the promotion_

post__ for the 1978 horror film *Piranha* feature__ an oversized piranha pois__ to bite the

_ of an unsuspect___ woman.

(2) **Write About the Photo**

Level 1

Level 2.

Level 3

(3) **Read, Then Write**

1. Describe the best birthday day celebration that you attended. What happened?

2. Describe a restaurant that you have recently enjoyed. What food did you order?

3. Describe a vacation that you appreciated. What did you do?

(4) Writing Sample (Short Essay).

1. Agree or disagree with this statement: Childhood obesity is an increasing problem in North America. As many as two-thirds of children are now obese. Explain your reasoning.

2. Agree or disagree with this statement: Success is often measured in terms of how much money somebody has earned. Explain your reasoning.

3. Agree or disagree with this statement: Honesty is the most import quality od a friend. Explain your reasoning.

Reading Tasks

1. Complete the Sentences

1. Some cities are calmly industrious, like Dusseldorf or Louisville. Others project an energy that they can hardly 1. _____, like New York or Hong Kong. And then you have Paris or Istanbul, and their patina full of 2. _____. Cities can be seen as living beings. Their space is 3. _____ by main streets and highways. At night these 4. _____ look dramatically red and golden. You can see the city's vascular system performing its 5. _____ function right before your eyes.

Drop down Menu choices to insert above

contain	vital	reworked	history	arteries	structured	displayed

2.

Human speech occurs without breaks. When one word ends and another begins, we don't actually pause to _____ the transition. When you listen to a recording of a language that you don't speak, you hear a continuous _____ of sounds that is more a warbling than a string of _____ words. We only learn when one-word stops and the next one starts over time, by _____ of certain verbal cues like inflection and stress patterns.

Drop down menu choices in insert above:

signal	link	stream	discernable	virtue	sound

3.

No one knows why the Roanoke settlers (1.)_____. Many people thought that (2.) _____ Native Americans killed them, but there were no signs of a (3.) ____. Some thought that the settlers died from hunger or disease, but they explain the (4.) _____ of the bodies. Today, the mystery remains unsolved.

Drop down menu choices in insert above:

absence	inexplicable	hostile	disappeared	argument	fight

2. Complete the Passage

Select the best sentence to fill in the blank in the passage:

1. During his lifetime, Shakespeare was very successful as a writer. This was mainly because of his genius. He knew how to write about life, and he had a wonderful way with words. In those days, the English were very interested in new ideas. They love music, art, plays, and poetry.	a. But Shakespeare success was also due to the special time when he lived. b. However, Shakespeare's words varied with the time of year. c. Shakespeare's plays lived on the stage. d. Shakespeare's English was different than Christopher Marlowe's.

Select the best sentence to fill in the blank in the passage:

2. A reaction that needs some type of energy to make it work is said to be endothermic. For example, if you put a mixture of baking soda and citric acid in your mouth, … It mixes with the moisture in your mouth an endothermic reaction occurs. It takes heat from your mouth and makes it feel cooler. Another example of an endothermic reaction is seen with cold packs used by athletes to treat injuries.	a. The warmer the reaction, the colder the feeling. b. The backpacks usually work to heat the wear's back. c. These packs usually consist of a plastic bag containing ammonium nitrate dissolved in water. d. Endothermic reactions are warm to touch, however.

The process of endothermic-taking heat energy from the surroundings and cooling the injured part of your body. In this way the cold pack acts as an ice pack It takes energy.	

Select the best sentence to fill in the blank in the passage:

3. When Dr. Charles Dance arrived at the foothills of the Appalachian Mountains in search of the sasquatch, he was widely ridiculed. Those who believed in the legendary creature told him he was over 2000 miles from where he ought to be looking, in eastern Idaho.	a. Another view concerns the map in which the doctor held.
	b. Others, who were more sceptical of the bipedal beast's existence, thought that Dr. Dance had finally lost his mind.
	c. Some thoughts that the sasquatch lived in Idaho mountains.
They demanded that his controversial Department of the Paranormal at Carolina Tech should be defunded immediately. Nevertheless, Dr. Dance pressed on with his field research, and no one could have predicted his remarkable findings.	d. Many people wanted to join his searches.

Highlight the Answer

.The Assyrians of the Sumerian period and the Egyptians of the same time recorded that willow ould be used to alleviate pain. Of course, these observations were made long before the advent of modern evidence-based medicine. And there fore the use of willow in ancient medicine had its oundations in observational or anecdotal vidence. Although physician from these times ad no way of understanding the mechanism by which willow bark might relieve pain, this lack of understanding did not stop them from prescribing this relatively safe and herbal remedy.	Click and drag text to highlight the answer to the question below: **What is the name of an early 'herbal remedy'?**

. The first mechanical clock probably emerged out of monasteries, developed by monks as alarms mechanisms to ring bells, according to the regular and regimented hours of their religious rituals. Once the twenty-four qual hour day was developed, the chiming of the bells gradually fell in line with the clock. early clocks, both large tower as well as turret ocks and the smaller models that they were used on, were propelled by weight echanisms. By the fifteenth century, however, the mainspring was developed, employing the stored power of a tightly coiled ring. This was soon followed by a devise	Click and drag text to highlight the answer to the question below: **What was advanced in the late 1300s and early 1400s?**

called the 'fusee', which equalized the momentum of a spring as it uncoiled. Smaller versions of this mechanism led to the invention of the watch.

---

3. Artificial corks and screw tops are the two main alternatives to natural wood corks. An artificial cork is made of ethylene vinyl acetate. It looks and feels very similar to real cork and a corkscrew is used to remove it from the bottle. It has two drawbacks: one is that it often fits so tight in the bottle that it is very difficult to remove (a problem that will no doubt be resolved through research). American wine producer, Alice Deacon, is more interested in the second, more technical problem. "We want to know whether the synthetic material is truly non-reactive and inert over long periods of time. Will it impart any tastes of its own to the wine?" Naturally, wineries using these plastic corks are deliberately aging wines to see what happens, but it is too soon by several years to know the outcome. Nonetheless, more and more low – and mid-range producers are switching to an artificial cork.

Click and drag text to highlight the answer to the question below:

What is the second problem with artificial corks mentioned in the passage?

4. Identify the Idea

1. But as a fine-art photographer I somehow felt that it wouldn't catch on out there, that there would be a problem with trying to make this as a fine-art career. And I kept being sucked into this genre of the calendar picture, or something of that nature, and I couldn't get away from it. So, I started to think of, how can I rethink the landscape? I decided to rethink the landscape as the landscape that we've transformed. I had a bit of an epiphany being lost in Pennsylvania, and I took a left turn trying to get back to the highway. And I ended up in a town called Frackville. I got out of the car, and I stood up, and it was a coal-mining town. I did a 360 turnaround, and that became one of the most surreal landscapes I've ever seen. Totally transformed by man. And that got me to go out and look at mines like this and go out and look at the largest industrial incursions in the landscape that I could find.	**Select the idea that is expressed in the passage.** a. The speaker was a fine artist who starting drawing landscapes of mines. b. The speaker was an industrial photographer that took 360-degree photographs. c. The speaker was a fine-art photographer who changed perspectives after observing a landscape surrounding a coalmine. d. The speaker was a fine-art photographer who investigated coalmining towns.

2. That's the interesting thing about work stress. We don't really experience much of it at work. We're too busy. We experience it outside of work, when we are commuting, when we're home, when we're trying to rejuvenate. It is important to recover in our spare time, to de-stress and do things we enjoy, and the biggest obstruction we face in that regard is ruminating. Because each time we do it, we're actually activating our stress response. Now, to ruminate means to chew over. It does not work for humans. Because what we chew over are the upsetting things, the distressing things, and we do it in ways that are entirely unproductive. It's the hours we spend obsessing about tasks we didn't complete or stewing about tensions with a colleague, or anxiously worrying about the future, or second-guessing decisions we've made.	**Select the idea that is expressed in the passage.** a. The speaker defines work stress as stress that people have while they are at work during working hours. b. The speaker defines work stress as the stress gained from talking to coworkers that do not understand them. c. The speaker defines work stress as destress. d. The speaker defines work stress as people who ruminate in completely unproductive ways outside of work hours.

3. The second half of the last century was completely defined by a technological revolution: the software revolution. The ability to program electrons on a material called silicon made possible technologies, companies and industries that were at one point unimaginable to many of us, but which have now fundamentally changed the way the world works. The first half of this century, though, is going to be transformed by a new software revolution: the living software revolution. And this will be powered by the ability to program biochemistry on a material called silicone. And doing so will enable us to harness the properties of biology to generate new kinds of therapies, to repair damaged tissue, to reprogram faulty cells or even build programmable operating systems out of biochemistry.

Select the idea that is expressed in the passage.

a. The speaker suggests that the first half of this century will be defined by soft cell revolution which includes, and we will be able to build programable pathologies.

b. The speaker suggests that the first half of this century will be defined by new software which will be able in which the speaker believes programable biochemistry will be able control biology in new ways.

c. The speaker believes that biochemistry and silicone chips will be a product of the next half century.

d. The speaker suggests that the first half of the next century will provide vast new insight into biochemistry and its uses.

5. Title the passage

1. More and more people are living to be 100 years old. In the United States there are more than 80,000 centenarians – 10 times more than there were 40 years ago. Professor Steven Heisler of Rockland University believes that future generations will live even longer, to 115 years and even more.	**Select the best title for the passage:** a. People are Living Longer! b. Rockland Prove It! c. Why not 200 years old! d. Live to be Old!

2. Vienna has a rich history. Its university started in 1365 and is one of the oldest in Europe. From 1557 to 1805 it was the centre of the Holy Roman Empire and it became an significant cultural centre of art and learning in the 18th and 19th centuries. The famous psychiatrist Sigmund Freud lived and worked here.	**Select the best title for the passage:** a. Vienna Today b. Freud's Home c. Roman Lives d. Vienna' History

3. The home of Jazz is often regarded as New Orleans. Jazz is a mixture of blues, dance songs, and hymns. Afro-American musicians started to play jazz in the late 19th century. Louis Armstrong and Jelly Roll Morton came from the city. Although the city is famous for its jazz music, it also has a philharmonic orchestra.	**Select the best title for the passage:** a. Home of the Blues b. Jelly Roll's city c. New Orleans is Jazz d. The New Orleans Philharmonic

Speaking Tasks

Read Aloud

Where is the bookshelf that we wanted?

How much did the monthly bus pass go up?

Multiplication and division are cornerstones of scientific study.

ee Duolingo on the blog at mjgeducation.com for more practice)

eak about a Photo

Level 1

Level 2

Level 3

91

2. Read, then Speak

1. Should television play a role in educating children? Why or why not?

2. What can we learn by studying events from the past?

3. What effects do you see of humans upon wild animals?

3. Listen, Then Speak

1. Tell me about the most interesting place in your hometown.

2. What is you favourite food? (Why?)

3. What type of films do you like best? (Why?)

Speaking Sample (Video)

1. What is the importance of travel to you?

   What types of people enjoy travelling?

   What do you think are the most popular holiday destinations?

   Would you like working overseas (why or why not)?

2. Describe a goal you have for yourself in the future

   What is your goal? (Answer this question first and then the finally 3 questions in any orde

   i. How do you plan to reach your goal?

   ii. When will you reach your goal?

   iii. Why is this goal important to you?

3. Describe something you own which is very important to you.

   i. What do you use it for?
   ii. How long you have had it?
   iii. Where did you get it from?
   iv. And explain why it is so important to you.

Listening Tasks

1. Listen and Select

Try the Duolingo Blog at mjgeducation.com for practice choosing 'real English words'.

2. Listen and Type

Try the Duolingo Blog at mjgeducation.com for practice typing complete sentences.

3. Listen, Then Speak

1. How much time do you spend with members of your family?
2. What kind of place would you like to live-in in the future?
3. How often do you go shopping and what do you buy?

Try the Duolingo Blog at mjgeducation.com for answering different questions.

Part 4 Answers

Answers to Part 3

Writing Parts

Read and Complete

Level 1

> Martin Luther King Jr. led many demonstrations against racism. He delivered his message in a non-violent manner. Some members of his movement later engaged in less peaceful protests. Luther King was detained several times.

Level 2

> Many parents believe that sugar consumption causes hyperactivity in their children. Indeed, 'sugar highs' are often blamed for rowdiness or excitability – but is sugar the guilty party, or is it simply a case of 'normal' childhood behaviour?

Level 3

> Despite the fact that piranhas are relatively harmless, many people continue to believe the pervasive myth that piranhas are dangerous to humans. This impression of piranhas is exacerbated by their mischaracterization in popular media. For example, the promotional poster for the 1978 horror film *Piranha* features an oversized piranha poised to bite the leg of an unsuspecting woman.

Write About the Photo

The directions for this task ask for 'one or more sentences that describe the image.', but you have only 1 minute to write. This is a perfect place TO SHOW OFF your knowledge of Sentence

Structure. Try to write 2 or 3 clauses, so a compound and complex sentences are most appropriate.

For the picture below:

This image shows the arm and hand of a courtroom judge, whose hand is holding a gavel, and we can see that he or she is striking the block at this given moment. The image is shot from the level of the desk, so nothing else can be seen but a desk lamp in the background. (56 words)

Level 1

For the picture below:

This image is of an Afro-American woman who is standing in the sunlight at the corner of a building. She has a red head dress on which is in contrast to the yellow corner of the building, but the head dress is colour coordinated with the sides of the building which are also red. (52 words)

Level 2.

For the image below:

The person in this image wearing a yellow shirt and blue jeans is photographed lifting the nose of a skateboard in mid-flight. We can assume that this person will complete the move and roll out of the tunnel where the picture has been taken. (44 words)

Level 3

Read, Then Write

Remember for this task you have 5 minutes to complete this task. You have to write at least 50 words as the test will indicate: "Respond to the question in at least 50 words". You will be able to see the question as you write, and your word count can be seen on the screen at all times.

Remember to use Paragraph form as in all the examples below (i.e., Topic sentence + Support + Detail/Examples, and a conclusion.

*Note: the easiest Topic sentence is to mention the Topic, add an adjective and then 'for several reasons' as below:

The **best (adjective)** *birthday party celebration was my own (Topic)* **for several reasons.** The 'reasons become the support sentences' – see below.

For example:

1. **Describe the best birthday day celebration that you attended. What happened?**

The best birthday party celebration was my own for several reasons. First, I was 7 years old, and my parents hired a clown. The seven friends I invited all laughed out loud at clown for about an hour. Also, the cake was special. The cake was made in the image of my favourite football team, Manchester United, and it had chocolate cake representation of David Beckham nd a large soccer ball made up of vanilla and chocolate icing. Finally, after a dinner of hamburgers and hotdogs, we danced to all the fun music we liked at the time. We almost forgot to open the presents! It was my best party because all my friends seemed to enjoy themselves as much as I did (an organized 123 words).

Describe a restaurant that you have recently enjoyed. What food did you order?

The Marble Slab restaurant where I had lunch with my girlfriend two weeks ago was very good for several reasons. First, when we entered the restaurant, we noticed it was very clean and light jazz music was playing at normal tempo. People were talking, but not too loud as to 'talk over' the music playing. Next, when we were seated, the waiter proved to be very kind and thoughtful, offering us the specials of the day and pouring us water before we ordered. Finally, the food was tremendous! My girlfriend ordered a salmon steak, and I ordered Beef Wellington. We shared our food between us because we both commented on the taste of our food. We are back for dinner in two weeks, just to see if the dinner could be better than our lunch (an organized 123 words).

Describe a vacation that you appreciated. What did you do?

In many ways, my cottage holiday last summer was one of the greatest vacations I ever had. Initially, I thought it was going to be boring alone in a cottage for 3 weeks, but it turned out to be a lot of fun. Everyday different people on the lake would drop by and ask if I would like to fish, water ski, or even go to town to get supplies. The cottage has been in my family for years, but I never realized how friendly everyone was on the lake. Even at night, we would play cards, listen to music, or even relax on the water taking a canoe ride. I was also invited out to dinner barbeques at other cottages several times. All-in-all, I came away for this vacation very relaxed and confident going back to work (an organized 138 words).

Writing Sample (Short Essay)

What a test-taker has to be conscious of is this that this 'writing Sample' is NOT graded but it i
sent on with your Report to the college or university you are applying to. The college or
university reads this sample to ensure that the potential student (you) can see/ argue both sides
an argument! This is made apparent as most questions are the Agree or Disagree type. So, there
are 3 ways you can answer this task in 3 to 5 minutes:

1. You can wholly agree.

2. You can wholly disagree.

3. You can argue using one side of the argument against the other (for the highest mark)

* Note: Write well 'to agree or disagree' can also provide a great score (quality response)

Each of these choices will be used in the questions that follow respectively.

1. **Agree or disagree with this statement: Childhood obesity is an increasing problem in
North America. As many as two-thirds of children are now obese. Explain your reasonin**

For example:

I completely **agree** with the statement above. Childhood obesity is on the rise for several
reasons.

(Body paragraph)

Parents should be responsible for their children, and this is probably the number one reason
why too many children are obese. Where else does a child learn their habits if not at home?
Too much food on the table and being told 'to eat' everything on their plate adds up! Another
reason that affects children is the amount of sugar they consume. Sugar is in almost everythir
in the stores these days, mostly in the drinks children consume. Finally, society is a fault as
well. Advertising directed at the childhood market makes for easy profits. These ads make
sugary foods and drinks to convincing by using cartoons, interesting music, and even
childhood celebrities. Kids then demand their parents buy these foods and drinks, so it is no
wonder there are more obese children these days.

(Conclusion)

In conclusion, parents, sugary foods and drinks, and advertising are the reasons there are more obese children these days. (An organized response of 170 words)

(Introduction)

2. Agree or disagree with this statement: Honesty is the most import quality of a friend. Explain your reasoning.

For example:

Although honesty is an important characteristic of a friend, I believe there are other qualities that are more important, such as integrity, loyalty, and being good listeners.

First of all, integrity in a friend, or strong moral principles, is important because there are many times a person needs a moral compass to do the right thing. For example, if I was thinking about gambling, a friend might persuade me to think about how hard I work for my money before I throw it away. Another characteristic that I admire is loyalty. If a friend stays with you through life's troubles, then he or she is loyal. Loyalty means a lot throughout your lifetime. Finally, being a good listener can help you solve a lot of problems. Many times, I need to explain my problems to others, but with nobody to listen to me, life can become frustrating.

In conclusion, since friends sent a lot of good times together, it is a true friend who can help through life's difficulties. (An organized response of 166 words)

. Agree or disagree with this statement: Success is often measured in terms of how much money somebody has earned. Explain your reasoning.

or example,

Although many people consider success to be the accumulation of a person's material wealth, there are other ways to measure a person's success.

There are several reasons why material wealth is a poor indicator of a person's success in life. One reason includes people who inherit their wealth from their family or win a lotto. These people should not be considered successful because they did not earn their money, yet in the public eye, they are usually considered successful.

Another way to measure a person's success is by how much they succeed to help people in society. Any person who sacrifices their time or money to help others may also be considered successful. Mother Teresa gave almost all of her time helping the poor in Bangladesh. She received a Nobel Peace as recognition.

In conclusion, success is essentially what people value most. In my opinion, social recognition is a better choice than material wealth because you are helping others, so the recognition is proof of success. (Organized 166 words)

Reading Parts

Complete the Sentences

For this task, please review Parts of Speech.

---

1. Some cities are calmly industrious, like Dusseldorf or Louisville. Others project an energy that they can hardly 1. _____, like New York or Hong Kong. And then you have Paris or Istanbul, and their patina full of 2. _____. Cities can be seen as living beings. Their space is 3. _____ by main streets and highways. At night these 4._____ look dramatically red and golden. You can see the city's vascular system performing its 5. _____ function right before your eyes.

---

contain	vital	reworked	history	arteries	structured	displayed

Kabbaj, W. (2016, September). What a driverless world could look like. Retrieved January 21, 2023, from https://www.ted.com/talks/wanis_kabbaj_what_a_driverless_world_could_look_like/transcript

- Remember to always read past the 'blank' to understand the full context of the sentence.

The parts of speech charts on the previous pages were constructed to make the test-taker, you, aware of the possibilities before you in Fill in the blanks in the reading section. When you scan the words at the bottom of the page before you start this exercise notice the possibilities for each word given. 'contain' can only be a verb, but can be used with modal verbs can or could or would; vital by its 'al' ending/suffix tells you it is a noun or an adjective; the words 'history' and arteries' are also nouns, though the latter is plural; the 'ed' ending/suffix for the words reworked, structured, and displayed have many possibilities: they can be a past participle (verb), they can be used with the verb to create passive sentences, they can also be adjectives in the 'ed' form. These possibilities can be winnowed down to correct answers by observing the grammar needed around the blank. At 1., 'can hardly' comes right in front of the blank. 'Can' is a modal form of a verb with an adverb hardly ('ly' suffix) that immediately follows it; therefore, the main verb is what has to fit in the blank. Since the words with the suffix 'ed' do not fit because following a modal verb like 'can' the main verb that follows never has a suffix – 'I did (auxiliary) <u>like</u> (main verb) the movie (I did <u>like</u> the movie); you can never add a suffix to the main verb after an auxiliary verb (I did not <u>liked</u> (X -wrong adding suffix –'ed' here) the movie). Thus, with this grammatical knowledge '<u>contain</u>' or 'can hardly <u>contain</u>' is the correct answer.

- **Note**: the opposing structure of the first sentences as well. The quiet cities vs. the louder cities. Opposing and parallel structures can also be clues that help find correct answers.

Grammar - context

At 2. A test-taker would look for a noun. There are no gerunds or present participles in the answer options, so we have to look for another noun that fits. The obvious answer is '<u>history</u>' as it relates to the context of the old cities Paris and Istanbul, whereas both arteries and vital do make any logical sense in this blank.

Grammar - meaning

At 3., although 'reworked' and 'displayed' have the same suffix as '<u>structured</u>', structured is the correct answer because it makes the most logical sense, or it is the most familiar answer by way of collocation. Other word possibilities have been used or do not fit by way of meaning or part of speech (suffix).

Grammar and collocation

At 4, only one word can fit in this blank that by context have to be 'red and golden' (thinking of time-lapse photography here): arteries. This is an example of an abstract meaning that can be used on the Duolingo exam. The word '<u>arteries</u>' stands out in the initial scan of words before you start to fill in the blanks because a test-taker would realize the context of the paragraph is about 'cities' – 'arteries' seems to be a strange word in the context of 'cities'. Yet, here, it is the only possible answer available, especially after you read the following sentence after the blank – 'You can see the cities vascular system…'; the words 'vascular system' ensure 'arteries' is the correct answer.

Abstract word

At 5., the only possible answer is '<u>vital</u>' as an adjective since 'reworked' and 'displayed' do not fit as context or meaning.

---

2. Human speech occurs without breaks. When one word ends and another begins, we don't actually pause to _____ the transition. When you listen to a recording of a language that

---

you don't speak, you hear a continuous _____ of sounds that is more a warbling than a string of _____ words. We only learn when one-word stops and the next one starts over time, by _____ of certain verbal cues like inflection and stress patterns.

| ink | discernible | virtue | signal | sound | stream |

onnikova, M. (2014, December 10). *Excuse me while I kiss this guy*. Retrieved January 23, 2023, from
ps://www.newyorker.com/science/maria-konnikova/science-misheard-lyrics-mondegreens

The parts of speech possibilities for these answer options are difficult. 'Link can be a verb or a noun. "Discernible is an adjective as told by its suffix 'ible'. Virtue is a noun. 'Signal' can be a verb, a noun, or an adjective in this form. Sound and stream can be either a noun or a verb.

1., signal or link can be used to complete this infinitive. 'Signal' is the correct choice simply because it sounds better than link, or you can think of 'link' as being slightly awkward in this blank. Other answer options, likewise, would sound awkward as well.

- Remember you do not have to do the blanks in the order that they read in the paragraph. It may be easier to skip one blank that has multiple possibilities in order to eliminate other words first, only to return and complete that blank at the end.

sound or collocation

2., the adjective 'continuous' helps place the word 'stream' 'of sounds' byway of collocation abstract/metaphoric usage of the word. This is a fairly common grouping of words often used linguistics.

abstract word or collocation or by elimination

3., test-takers would notice the blank falls in front of a noun 'words'; therefore, an adjective is needed in this blank. Between the words 'signal' and 'discernible', discernible is the correct answer because 'signal words' does not logically fit into the blank.

grammar and logic

4., the only logical word to fit in the blank would be the noun 'virtue' as all other choices do logically fit into the blank.

3. More than half of the world's population already lives in cities, and another 2.5 billion people are 1. _____ to move to urban areas by 2050. The way we build new cities will be at the 2. _____ of so much that matters, from climate change to economic 3. _____ to our very well-being and sense of connectedness. We need to be planning the cities of the future now, and we need to be 4. _____ for a design that is focused on human interaction.

advocating	vitality	heart	end	planned	projected

Calthorpe, P. (2017, April). *7 principles for building better cities*. Retrieved January 23, 2020, from https://www.ted.com/talks/peter_calthorpe_7_principles_for_building_better_cities

The scan of the words below the text reveals their possibilities as parts of speech to fill in the blanks. 'Advocating' as a gerund can be a noun, it can also be used in combination with the ver 'to be' to create the present progressive verb tense, or it can be an adjective. 'Vitality' by its 'it suffix is a noun, 'heart' is a noun – but seems out of place in the context of 'cities'. 'End' is a noun. 'Planned' and projected can be adjectives, past participles to be used in conjunction to create the passive 'to be' (is/are planned/projected, has been planned/projected) or as different verb tenses – (has/have planned/projected, etc.).

At 1., either 'planned' or 'projected' is the right answer as both can be used in this passive fore with 'are'. However, 'projected' is the correct answer because 'planned' does logically fit (are planning would be better)

Grammar- meaning

At 2., either 'heart' or 'end' can fit, but 'at the end of so much that matters' does not ring true with 'at the heart of so much that matters', so 'heart' is the correct answer.

- Notice the metaphoric use of the word heart. As a noun, we think of the organ that pumps blood in the middle of our chest. As a metaphor, it is being used as a 'central location' or 'in the middle' of 'so much that matters'.

Abstract word

At 3., the word needed is a noun, because economic is being used as an adjective in front of th blank, so 'vitality' is the proper choice as the other words have difficulty making any logical sense in this blank. You can tell 'vitality' is a noun by its suffix 'ity'. You may also notice that 'economic vitality' is a fairly common collocation in business pages of newspapers and magazines.

Grammar and collocation

At 4., notice the parallel structure of both clauses in this sentence: 'we need to be'. Notice in the first clause a gerund 'planning' is used, so it logically follows that in this parallel structure a second gerund would be used in the second clause. Thus, 'advocating' is the correct answer. It can also be surmised that none of the other answer options would fill this blank.

Complete the Passage

1. During his lifetime, Shakespeare was very successful as a writer. This was mainly because of his genius. He knew how to write about life, and he had a wonderful way with words.	Select the best sentence to fill in the blank in the passage:
	a. **But Shakespeare success was also due to the special time when he lived.**
* (Fill this space with the correct sentence)	b. However, Shakespeare's words varied with the time of year.
	c. Shakespeare's plays lived on the stage.
In those days, the English were very interested in new ideas. They love music, art, plays, and poetry.	d. Shakespeare's English was different than Christopher Marlowe's.

Answer 'A' is correct because it refers to 'the special time' and the following sentence refers to in those days' – referring to 'time' again. Answers B, C, D do not follow logically and are distractions from the correct answer A even though they are coherent sentences, they do not fit into the paragraph reasonably.

2. A reaction that needs some type of energy to make it work is said to be endothermic. For example, if you put a mixture of baking soda and citric acid in your mouth, … It mixes with the moisture in your mouth and an endothermic reaction occurs. It takes heat from your mouth and makes it feel cooler. Another example of an endothermic reaction is seen with cold packs used by athletes to treat injuries. *** (Fill this space with the correct sentence)** The process of endothermic-taking heat energy from the surroundings and cooling the injured part of your body. In this way the cold pack acts as an ice pack. Select the best sentence to fill in the blank in the passage:	Select the best sentence to fill in the blank in the passage: a. The warmer the reaction, the colder the feeling. b. The backpacks usually work to heat the wear's back. c. **These packs usually consist of a plastic bag containing ammonium nitrate dissolved in water.** d. Endothermic reactions are warm to touch, however.

Answer C is correct since it is the only response that refers back to the 'cold packs', so it fits logically into the paragraph, whereas the other answers do not.

3. When Dr. Charles Dance arrived at the foothills of the Appalachian Mountains in search of the sasquatch, he was widely ridiculed. Those who believed in the legendary creature told him he was over 2000	Select the best sentence to fill in the blank in the passage: a. Another view concerns the map in which the doctor held.

| miles from where he ought to be looking, in eastern Idaho.

* (Fill this space with the correct sentence)

They demanded that his controversial Department of the Paranormal at Carolina Tech should be defunded immediately. Nevertheless, Dr. Dance pressed on with his field research, and no one could have predicted his remarkable findings. | **b. Others, who were more sceptical of the bipedal beast's existence, thought that Dr. Dance had finally lost his mind.**

c. Some thoughts that the sasquatch lived in Idaho mountains.

d. Many people wanted to join his searches. |

Answer B is correct because the sentence that begins with 'Those that believed' setting up the following sentence 'Others...though' as though the writer is suggesting of the 2 main opposing groups to the doctor's search. The other answers are not grammatically correct, however.

Highlight the Answer (answers are in bold text)

| 1.The Assyrians of the Sumerian period and the Egyptians of the same time recorded that willow could be used to alleviate pain. Of course, these observations were made long before the advent of modern evidence-based medicine. And, therefore, the use of willow in ancient medicine had its foundations in observational or anecdotal evidence. Although physician from these times had no way of understanding the mechanism by which **willow bark** might relieve pain, this | Click and drag text to highlight the answer to the question below:

What is the name of the early 'herbal remedy' mentioned in the text? |

lack of understanding did not stop them from prescribing this relatively safe and herbal remedy.	

2. The first mechanical clock probably emerged out of monasteries, developed by monks as alarms mechanisms to ring bells, according to the regular and regimented hours of their religious rituals. Once the twenty-four equal hour day was developed, the chiming of the bells gradually fell in line with the clock. Early clocks, both large tower as well as turret clocks and the smaller models that they were based on, were propelled by weight mechanisms. **By the fifteenth century, however, the mainspring was developed**, employing the stored power of a tightly coiled spring. This was soon followed by a devise called the 'fusee', which equalized the momentum of a spring as it uncoiled. Smaller versions of this mechanism led to the invention of the watch.	Click and drag text to highlight the answer to the question below: **What was advanced in the late 1300s and early 1400s?**

. Artificial corks and screw tops are the two main alternatives to natural wood corks. An artificial cork is made of ethylene vinyl acetate. It looks and feels very similar to real cork and a corkscrew is used to remove it from the bottle. It has two drawbacks: one is that it often fits so tight in the bottle that it is very difficult to remove (a problem that will no doubt be resolved through research). American wine producer, Alice Deacon, is more interested in the second, more technical problem. **"We want to know whether the synthetic material is truly non-reactive and inert over long periods of time.** Will it impart any tastes of its own to the wine?" Naturally, wineries using these plastic corks are deliberately aging wines to see what happens, but it is too soon by several years to know the outcome. Nonetheless, more and more low – and mid-range producers are switching to an artificial cork.

Click and drag text to highlight the answer to the question below:

What is the second problem with artificial corks mentioned in the passage?

Identify the Idea

	Select the idea that is expressed in the passage
1. But as a fine-art photographer I somehow felt that it wouldn't catch on out there, that there would be a problem with trying to make this as a fine-art career. And I kept being sucked into this genre of the calendar picture, or something of that nature, and I couldn't get away from it. So, I started to think of, how can I rethink the landscape? I decided to rethink the landscape as the landscape that we've transformed.	a. The speaker was a fine artist who starting drawing landscapes of mines.
	b. The speaker was a industrial photographer that took 360 degree photographs.
	c. The speaker was a fine-art photographe who changed perspectives after observing landscape, surrounding a coalmine.
I had a bit of an epiphany being lost in Pennsylvania, and I took a left turn trying to get back to the highway. And I ended up in a town called Frackville. I got out of the car, and I stood up, and it was a coal-mining town. I did a 360 turnaround, and that became one of the most surreal landscapes I've ever seen. Totally transformed by man. And that got me to go out and look at mines like this and go out and look at the largest industrial incursions in the landscape that I could find.	d. The speaker was a fine-art photographer who investigated coalmining towns.

Answer c is correct. No topic sentence, so piece together the main idea by way of context.

2. That's the interesting thing about work stress. We don't really experience much of it at work. We're too busy. We experience it outside of work, when we are commuting, when we're home, when we're trying to rejuvenate. It is important to recover in our spare time, to de-stress and do things we enjoy, and the biggest obstruction we face in that regard is ruminating. Because each time we do it, we're actually activating our stress response. Now, to ruminate means to chew over. It does not work for humans. Because what we chew over are the upsetting things, the distressing things, and we do it in ways that are entirely unproductive. It's the hours we spend obsessing about tasks we didn't complete or stewing about tensions with a colleague, or anxiously worrying about the future, or second-guessing decisions we've made.	**Select the idea that is expressed in the passage** a. The speaker defines work stress as stress that people have while they are at work during working hours. b. The speaker defines work stress as the stress gained from talking to coworkers that do not understand them. c. The speaker defines work stress as distress. d. **The speaker defines work stress as people who ruminate in completely unproductive ways outside of work hours.**

Answer d is correct. Topic sentence answers tells of the main idea... "We experience it outside of work, when we are commuting, when we're home, when we're trying to rejuvenate." **Repeated paraphrase outside work hours = outside work; unproductive hours paraphrased as** "when we are commuting, when we're home, when we're trying to rejuvenate."

3. The second half of th ⸱ry was completely defined by a technological revolution: the software revolution. The ability to program electrons on a material called silicon made possible technologies, companies and industries that were at one point unimaginable to many of us, but which have now fundamentally changed the way the world works. The first half of this century, though, is going to be transformed by a new software revolution: the living software revolution. And this will be powered by the ability to program biochemistry on a material called biology. And doing so will enable us to harness the properties of biology to generate new kinds of therapies, to repair damaged tissue, to reprogram faulty cells or even build programmable operating systems out of biochemistry.	**Select the idea that is expressed in the passage** a. The speaker suggests that the first half of this century will be defined by soft cell revolution which includes biology, and we will be able to build programable pathologies. b. **The speaker suggests that the first half of this century will be defined by new software whereby programable biochemistry will be able control biology in new ways.** c. The speaker believes that biochemistry and silicone chips will be a product of the next half-century. d. The speaker suggests that the first half of the next century will provide vast new insight into biochemistry and its uses.

Answer B is correct and can be found by locating the topic sentence: "The first half of this century, though, is going to be transformed by a new software revolution: the living software revolution." The main idea is about the future, not the past.

Title the passage (answers should be obvious)

1. More and more people are living to be 100 years old. In the United States there are more than 80,000 centenarians – 10 times more than there were 40 years ago. Professor Steven Heisler of Rockland University believes that future generations will live even longer to 115 years and even more.	**Select the best title for the passage** a. **People are Living Longer!** b. Rockland Prove It! c. Why not 200 years old! d. Live to be Old!

2. Vienna has a rich history. Its university started in 1365 and is one of the oldest in Europe. From 1557 to 1805 it was the centre of the Holy Roman Empire and it became an significant cultural centre of art and learning in the 18th and 19th centuries. The famous psychiatrist Sigmund Freud lived and worked here.	**Select the best title for the passage** a. Vienna Today b. Freud's Home c. Roman Lives d. **Vienna' History**

3. The home of Jazz is often regarded as New Orleans. Jazz is a mixture of blues, dance songs, and hymns. Afro-American musicians started to play jazz in the late 19th century. Louis Armstrong and Jelly Roll Morton came from the city. Although the city is famous for its jazz music, it also has a philharmonic orchestra.	**Select the best title for the passage** a. Home of the Blues b. Jelly Roll's city c. **New Orleans is Jazz** d. The New Orleans Philharmonic

Answers to the Part 3

Speaking Parts

Read Aloud (20 seconds to Record (Read) one sentence)

1. Where is the bookshelf that we wanted?

2. How much did the monthly bus pass go up?

3. Multiplication and division are cornerstones of scientific study.

(See Duolingo blog at mjgeducation.com for more practice)

Speak about a Photo

Duolingo demands Speaking for at least 30 seconds about an image (1:30 max.). The idea is to describe the image to an imaginary person, a person who cannot see the image.

1. State what it is or what is happening first

2. If the image has depth, ad one sentence about the foreground and a sentence about the background.

3. If no depth (as with picture 1 here), talk about detail colour, size, material etc.

4. Finally, add a potential future or personal 'desire' about the image.

Note*: (Use normal speech, so you will probably pause a little before you speak)

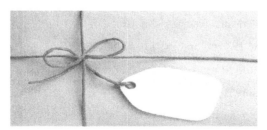

1. Level 1

For the above picture:

can see what looks to be a package. It has a red cord tied around the length and width that ends in a bow. The packaging is brown paper, which looks like typical packaging material. There is a tag on the end of the red cord, but there is no name on it. I hope this package gets mailed to me (or 'I wonder what is in this package').

Level 2

r the above picture:

This is an image of a barber cutting a man's hair. In the foreground, I can see the left hand of the barber holding a small black comb, and the right hand is holding scissors as he trims round the man's ear. The man in the chair has a beard and a dark blue apron around his neck. In the background, I can make out empty barber chairs.

Level 3

r the above picture:

This picture depicts 6 medical people standing in a hallway, probably in a hospital. In the foreground, in the centre of the picture seems to be a doctor. He looks like a doctor because he wearing a white coat and a stethoscope around his neck. The other people in the picture in the background look to be nurses because they are wearing blue scrubs – 4 are women and the other person is a man. They are all smiling, too. Maybe they have just saved a person's life!

Read, then Speak

For this task, you have 30 to 1:30 seconds to answer 1 question and several sub-questions. Try to open with a topic sentence and give examples/ detail for each question.

1. **What is the importance of travel to you?**

   What types of people enjoy travelling?

   What do you think are the most popular holiday destinations?

For example:

Travel is important to me for several reasons. For example, I can relax and forget about my troubles for a little while, learn about a new culture, and meet interesting people. On my last vacation, I went to North Carolina and spent a lot of time near the beach and visiting places in Raleigh, the capital city.

I think young and old people like to travel most for a couple of reasons. First, seniors probably have more money than others, so they can afford to travel, and young people because they are so interested in seeing the world.

The most popular destinations are beaches, I believe. Everybody wants to sit on warm beaches, possibly because they live in colder climates.

2. **Describe a goal you have for yourself in the future**

   What is your goal? (Answer this question first and then the finally 3 questions in any order

i. How do you plan to reach your goal?

ii. When will you reach your goal?

iii. Why is this goal important to you?

For example:

I want to be a teacher in the future. I am in my first year of university, so after my second year, I can choose to study education and study toward being a teacher. I will have to study to get high grades because there is a certain 'honors' level I have to maintain, and after three years I will be certified as a teacher. I will also have to choose to teach elementary or high school students by my final year. So, if all goes well and I do not change my mind, I will be a teacher in 4 more years.

I have wanted to be a teacher since I enjoyed my high school teachers so much. I learned a great deal and I think that this would be a great job because I can teach and help students and have my summers off, too!

3. **Describe something you own which is very important to you.**

i. What do you use it for?

ii. How long you have had it?

iii. Where did you get it from?

iv. And explain why it is so important to you.

I have a watch that my grandfather gave to me that was given to him by his grandfather. This watch is the kind you tuck in your pocket because it is attached by a gold chain – an old style of watch. It is over 100 years old now as you can see that the metal is worn down. My grandfather passed away about 10 years ago and he gave it to me about 2 years before that. I do not use it very much even though it still works. It is in my bedroom desk drawer, but I take it out now and then just to look at it and think about my grandfather. It is a family heirloom now, so I imagine I will pass it on to my children or my children's children someday.

Speaking Sample (Video)

The prompt says, **'Speak for 1 to 3 minutes about the topic below'.** This is the most difficult task to complete because you have to speak for such a long time. This task is not graded but, as I mentioned previously, it is passed on to the college and university you have/will apply to. There is no pressure, on the one hand, because it is not being scored; however, if speak well for approximately 2:00 minutes it could help you be accepted. Why? Well, just like your written sample, the school administration wants to see that their potential entrants can organize a proper response – that is all! If you are organized, you will be accepted. I know that I have mentioned this many times in this text, but after 20 years of tertiary education teaching, I know this to be fact. So, speak in paragraph form and give a lot of examples/ detail about the topic, which will help get you over the 2-minute threshold – 2 minutes will ensure you have given a satisfying response.

1. Speak at a normal pace. You can pause, but not too long.

2. Organize around topic sentences and give examples/detail, but do not tell stories unless they are entirely relevant to your topic.

3. Make up a response if you have to but enjoy it – have fun when your respond.

4. Try to give at least 3 examples for each topic (practice this before the test!)

* Remember the prompts/questions are designed to 'open', so you can give a long response....but you have to 'control'/organize your response.

5. Use Signal words to help organize your response – first, also, next, initially, finally, last etc.

From the Duolingo website from the Speaking Sample:

1. Who is a person you think you have impacted in your life? What impact have you had on that person, and how?

11

Response

> The person I believe I have influenced the most is my younger brother. My younger brother is 3 years younger than me, and ever since I can remember he has followed me around, so from a very young age I have realized I was a kind of teacher to him.
>
> - When was 7, I taught him how to swim.
> - When he was 8, I helped teach him how to ice skate
> - When he was 10, I showed him how to catch a football etcetera...
>
> So, he always admired me because I showed him how to do things, even math, and writing. I am pretty much a straight person; I mean I go home after school, I am in high school now, and do my homework. If I play baseball, hockey, or football, I do it when the coach tells us or after dinner. I can see my brother following the same schedule, and playing the same sports as I do. I can say that I have impacted him in these ways. He is now realizing there are other things that he likes to do but he follows the same approach as I do, so he is on his own, but I think I have influenced him a lot. Morally, too. I still go to church on Sundays, and he does, too. So whenever a 'moral problem' comes up – what is the right thing to do question – we have the teachings of the church to help remind us of the 'right' course of action.
> He is my brother, so I guess I will always be there to help him.

2. **Do you think that young adults should pay rent to their parents if they do not move out by the age of 21? Explain your reasons.**

Outline:

Topic sentence: I believe that young adults have a right to stay home for as long as they want without paying rent. The basis of this response is upon employment.

Reason 1: First, to have a job means that you have an income and can afford to pay rent.

119

Detail: But, if you do not have a job, there is no way to pay rent to your parents – and your parents certainly do not want you to live on the streets.

Reason 2: Also, if a 21-year-old has a job, they probably want to move out of the house immediately, anyway.

Detail: Most people I know leave home when they graduate from high school or university. Parents have to give their children a chance to graduate from university or college before asking for any kind of rent money.

Reason 3: Finally, parents should allow their children to stay home past the age of 21 if they are employed because they need to save a little money before they start paying rent in their own apartments.

Detail: Most apartment rentals ask for the first and last month's rent.

Conclusion: For these reasons, young adults need their parent's support.

Response:

I believe that young adults have a right to stay home for as long as they want without paying rent. The basis of this response is upon employment. If a 21-year-old has a job, then I think they can pay some rent. If they are not employed, then they should not have to pay any rent – and their parents should understand that. First, to have a job means that you have an income and can afford to pay rent. But, if you do not have a job, there is no way to pay rent to your parents – and your parents certainly do not want you to live on the streets. Also, if a 21-year-old has a job, they probably want to move out of the house immediately, anyway. Most people I know leave when they graduate from high school or university. Parents have to give their children a chance to graduate from university or college before asking for any kind of rent money. Finally, parents should allow their children to stay home past the age of 21 if they are employed because they need to save a little money before they start paying rent in their own apartments. Most apartment rentals ask for the first and last month's rent. For these reasons, young adults need their parent's support.

Do you think all university students should study abroad for a year, if there is sufficient funding? <u>Explain your reasons.</u>

utline your ideas in your head (3 reasons):

>pic sentence: I believe that university students should study overseas for several reasons.

Reason 1: First, it is all about culture.

- **Detail**: Students can learn a great deal by being immersed in a different culture where they can expand their knowledge of different traditions and languages of a different culture. This can be a lot of fun because it is so interesting to be apart of Christmas, festivals, or rituals.

Reason 2: Also, studying overseas allows students to observe different professors and instructors that have different study methods.

- **Detail**: There are usually many ways of getting to the same answer, so this can be accelerated by studying under foreign instructors. Elon Musk chose to study in Canada even though he is from South Africa.

Reason 3: Finally, studying abroad helps students find employment after they graduate.

- **Detail**: Many employers seek for employees with experience in multicultural environments, so education counts

Conclusion: In these ways, studying overseas can be beneficial for students.

sponse:

believe that university students should study overseas for several reasons. **First**, it is all
>out culture. Students can learn a great deal by being immersed in a different culture where
ey can expand their knowledge of different traditions and languages of a different culture.
nis can be a lot of fun because it is so interesting to be a part of Christmas, festivals, or
:uals. **Also**, studying overseas allows students to observe different professors and instructors
at have different study methods. Detail: There are usually many ways of getting to the same

answer, so this can be accelerated by studying under foreign instructors. Elon Musk chose to study in Canada even though he is from South Africa. **Finally**, studying abroad helps students find employment after they graduate. Many employers seek employees with experience in multicultural environments, so education counts. **In these ways, studying overseas can be beneficial for students.**

Listening Tasks:

Listening Practice can be found at mjgeducation.com – Blog – type Duolingo for all videos.

Part 5

Topical Questions to practice for the Speaking and Writing Tasks

This is a list of topics and questions that possibly turn up on the Duolingo exam. However, they are more important as practice to help develop your topic sentences when Speaking and Writing. The topic is given, so you have to provide a controlling idea…. and then progress to Support sentences and then examples/detail towards a conclusion. If you practice this technique, the Duolingo's productive skill tasks will become much easier.

Speaking Tasks: Speak about the Photo, Read and Speak, Listen, Then Speak, and the Speaking Sample.

Writing Tasks: Write about the Photo, Read Then Write, and the Writing Sample.

Advice

What three pieces of advice will you give your children?

Whose advice do you follow more, your parents' or your friends' advice?

What are some things students should do to improve their English?

Appearance

What is the first thing you notice about a person?

What do the clothes someone wears say about that person?

Art

How often do you go to art museums?

Do you consider yourself to be artistic?

What do you think about modern art paintings?

Cities

Do you like cities or the countryside? Which is better and why?

You can make one change to your city, what will you change?

What are some of most famous cities in the world? What makes them famous?

Color

What is your favorite color?

Is color important to you?

Does color affect your emotions?

Cooking

How often do you cook?

How good are you at cooking?

What are some things that you can cook?

Crime

Is shoplifting common in your country?

What do you think the most common crime in your country is?

Should police in your country be stricter or less strict?

Dreaming

How often do you dream?

D Do you think dreams have meanings?

Do you dream in color or black and white?

Eating Habits

Talk about what you have eaten today.

What is the unhealthiest food you can think of?

What do people need to eat more of?

Electric Cars

Would you ever drive an electric car?

What are some of the benefits and disadvantages of electric cars?

Environmental Problems

What are some of the most serious environmental problems?

What are 3 things governments can do to help the environment?

Family Values

What values will you pass on to your children?

Do you think society is losing its values?

Friendship

Do you prefer to have many friends or just a few that you are close to?

What are the benefits of having just a few close friends? How about the benefits of having many friends?

Describe your best friend.

Getting a Job

What is the best way to find a job?

What do you think are the five most common questions asked at a job interview?

What are some things you should do for a job interview? How about things you shouldn't do?

Habits

What are some things you do every day?

What are some good habits you have?

Do you have any bad habits?

Individuality

What makes you unique?

Is it okay to look different from other people or should you look the same as other people?

What do you think when you see someone who looks very different?

Intelligence

Can intelligence be measured? If so, what is the best way to measure it? If not, why not?

What is the most intelligent animal?

Do you think that intelligence is only based on genetics or can things in a child's environment boost intelligence?

Jobs

What are some of the worst jobs you can think of?

What are some of the best jobs you can think of?

How long do you want to work?

Languages

Which languages are the most difficult to learn?

Which languages are the easiest to learn?

Love

Do you believe that love can be understood by looking at the brain and chemicals?

How is attraction different than love?

In public, how much affection is too much?

Manners

What are some examples of bad manners on the bus?

What are some examples of good manners on the subway?

What are some examples of bad manners that you dislike?

Meeting New People

If you don't know your partners very well, ask them some questions to get to know them.

Do you like meeting new people? Why or why not?

Motivation

What motivates you? Why?

Are you very motivated to do things or do you need motivation?

What activity do you have no motivation to do?

Music

Who are your favorite bands or artists?

How often do you listen to music?

When was the last time you bought a song or album?

News

Where do you get your news from?

How important is it for people to follow the news?

Do you think that news agencies sometimes tell lies to make a story more popular?

Personality

Describe your personality.

What kinds of people do you get along well with?

What kinds of personality traits do you dislike?

Responsibility

How involved should governments be in individuals' lives?

Are criminals ever NOT responsible for the crimes they commit?

What responsibilities do university students have? How about children or adults?

Success and Failure

Success

Describe a successful person.

Is your idea of success the same as your parents' idea of success?

Failure

Have there been any failures that made your life better?

Can you think of any famous people who failed spectacularly at something?

Technology

Talk about how technology has changed in your lifetime.

What do you think has been the most important new invention in the last 100 years?

What do you think will be the next biggest technological advance?

The Five Senses

What is your favorite sense? Give some examples why it is so good.

If you had to lose one sense, which would it be?

What is the most wonderful smell?

Part 6

Vocabulary

The words below range from 1 to 7 syllable words with short definitions that may help you vary your vocabulary while Speaking or Writing.

For words in better Context (**VERY IMPORTANT) or organized in groups, test-takers can try a picture dictionary:

1. https://www.opdome.com/

2. http://www.vidtionary.com/ (Video)

3. https://www.youtube.com/c/Oxfordpicturedictionary (on YouTube)

4. https://www.visualdictionaryonline.com/society.php

1. Syllable:
1. Dross (noun)- something that is base, trivial, or inferior
2. Pan (verb) - to criticize severely
3. Bilk (verb) - to obtain (something) by defrauding someone
4. Wax (intransitive verb) - to assume a (specified) characteristic, quality, or state: wax indignant
5. Shard (noun) - a piece or fragment of a brittle substance
6. Niche (noun) - a specialized market, a place for something
7. Scourge (noun) - an instrument of punishment or criticism

2. Syllables:
1. Fiat (noun) - a command or act of will that creates something without or as if without further effort
2. Hubris (noun) - exaggerated pride or self-confidence
3. Elan (noun) - vigorous spirit or enthusiasm
4. Tacit (adjective) -expressed or carried on without words or speech
5. Panache (noun) - dash or flamboyance in style and action
6. Acute (adjective) - marked by keen discernment or intellectual perception especially of subtle distinctions
7. Obtuse (adjective) - lacking sharpness or quickness of sensibility or intellect
8. Astute (adjective) - mentally sharp or clever
9. Zeitgeist (noun) - the general intellectual, moral, and cultural climate of an era

10. Chthonic (adjective) - of or relating to the underworld

11. Delta (noun) - the <u>alluvial</u> deposit at the mouth of a river

12. Hoary (adjective) - gray or white with or as if with age

13. Nuance (noun) - a <u>subtle</u> distinction or variation

14. Impasse (noun) - a <u>predicament affording</u> no obvious escape

15. Schism (noun) - a formal division in or separation from a church or religious body

16. Dilate (intransitive verb) - to become wide

17. Latent (adjective) - present and capable of emerging or developing but not now visible, obvious, active

3. Syllables:

1. Adamant (adjective) - unshakable or <u>insistent</u> especially in maintaining a position or opinion

2. Liminal (adjective) - of, relating to, or situated at a sensory threshold: barely perceptible or capable of eliciting a response

3. Patina (noun) - a surface appearance of something grown beautiful especially with age or use

4. Cavalier (adjective) - marked by or given to offhand and often disdainful dismissal of important matters

5. Tenebrous (adjective) - shut off from the light

6. Scintilla (noun) - spark or trace

7. Acumen (noun) - keenness and depth of perception

8. Sagacious (adjective) - keen and farsighted <u>penetration</u> and judgment

9. Discerning (adjective) - showing <u>insight</u> and understanding

10. Cognizant (adjective) - knowledgeable of something especially through personal experience

11. Prescient (noun) - foreknowledge of events

12. Prosaic (adjective) - differentiated from poetry; dull unimaginative

13. Mnemonic (adjective) - assisting or intended to assist memory

14. Didactic (adjective) - designed or intended to teach

15. Erudite (adjective) - having or showing knowledge that is gained by studying

16. Judicious (adjective) - having, exercising, or characterized by sound judgment

17. Tectonics (noun) - a branch of geology concerned with the structure of the crust of a planet, especially with the formation of folds and faults in it

18. Libido (noun) – instinctual psychic energy that in psychoanalytic theory is derived from primitive biological urges; sexual energy

19. Expiate (verb) - to make amends for

20. Mountebank (noun) - a boastful unscrupulous pretender

21. Misnomer (noun) - a use of a wrong or inappropriate name

22. Virago (noun) - a loud overbearing woman; shrew

23. Dogmatic (adjective) - characterized by or <u>given</u> to the expression of opinions very strongly or positively as if they were facts

24. Abrogate (verb) - to abolish by <u>authoritative</u> action or annul

25. Conundrum (noun) - an <u>intricate</u> and difficult problem
26. Obfuscate (verb) - to throw into shadow; darken
27. Postmodern (adjective) - various movements in reaction to modernism that are typically characterized by a return to traditional materials and forms (as in architecture) or by ironic self-reference and absurdity (as in literature)
28. Palimpsest (noun) - writing material (such as a parchment or tablet) used one or more times after earlier writing has been erased
29. Cynosure (noun) - one that serves to direct or guide
30. Paradox (noun) - a statement that is seemingly <u>contradictory</u> or opposed to <u>common sense</u> and yet is perhaps true
31. Narcissist (noun) - an extremely self-centered person who has an exaggerated sense of self-importance
32. Redundant (adjective) - <u>exceeding</u> what is necessary or normal
33. Enigma (noun) - something hard to understand or explain
34. Visceral (adjective) - felt in or as if in the internal organs of the body
35. Inculcate (verb) - to teach and impress by frequent repetitions or admonitions
36. Dyspeptic (noun) – indigestion; ill humour
37. Sobriquet (noun) - a descriptive name or epithet or nickname
38. Prescience (noun) - human anticipation of the course of events

4. <u>Syllables</u>:

1. Assiduous (adjective) - showing great care, attention, and effort
2. Apocryphal (adjective) - of <u>doubtful</u> authenticity; spurious
3. Ineffable (adjective) - incapable of being expressed in words
4. Iridescent (adjective) - having properties of iridescence or a lustrous rainbowlike play of color caused by differential refraction of light waves
5. Casuistry (noun) - a resolving of specific cases of conscience, duty, or conduct through an interpretation of ethical principles or religious doctrine
6. Lilliputian (adjective) – small or miniature (ref. Gulliver's Travels by Jonathan Swift)
7. Symbiotic (adjective) - characterized by, living in, or being a close physical association
8. Polysemous (adjective) - having multiple meanings
9. Avaricious (adjective) - greedy of gain: excessively acquisitive especially in seeking to hoard riches
10. Hermeneutics (noun) - the study of the <u>methodological</u> principles of interpretation
11. Empirical (adjective) - originating in or based on observation or experience
12. Hortatory (adjective) - urging to some course of conduct or action; exhorting; encouraging
13. Concomitant (adjective) – accompanying, especially in a subordinate or <u>incidental</u> way
14. Impunity (noun) - exemption or freedom from punishment, harm, or loss
15. Hegemony (noun) - influence or authority over others

16. Labyrinthine (adjective) - related to a labyrinth: a place constructed of or full of intricate passageways and blind alleys

17. Jeremiad (noun) - a prolonged lamentation or complaint

18. Microcosm (noun) - a little world

19. Attenuate (verb) - to lessen the amount, force, magnitude, or value; to weaken

20. Rebarbative (adjective) – repellent or irritating

21. Dialectic (noun) - the Socratic techniques of exposing false beliefs and eliciting truth

22. Doppelganger (noun) – double; alter ego; a person's twin

23. Oxymoron (noun) - a combination of contradictory or incongruous words (such as *cruel kindness*

24. Ambivalent (adjective) - having or showing simultaneous and contradictory attitudes or feelings toward something or someone

25. Simulacrum (noun) – a representation; an insubstantial form or semblance of something

26. Tautology (noun) - needless repetition of an idea, statement, or word

27. Ambiguous (adjective) - doubtful or uncertain especially from obscurity or indistinctness

28. Reiterate (verb) - to state or do over again or repeatedly sometimes with wearying effect

29. Iconoclast (noun) - a person who attacks settled beliefs or institutions

30. Exegesis (noun) - explanation, exposition

31. Dionysian (adjective) - characteristic of Dionysus or the cult of worship of Dionysus: being of a frenzied or orgiastic character

32. Exiguous (adjective) - excessively scanty

33. Draconian (adjective) – cruel, severe; a severe code of laws

34. Peremptory (adjective) - putting an end to or precluding a right of action, debate, or delay

35. Solipsistic (adjective) - extreme egocentricity

5. Syllables:

1. Inexorable (adjective) - not to be persuaded, moved, or stopped
2. Hebetudinous (adjective) – suggestive of a person's mental dullness, often marked by laziness or torpor
3. Apollonian (adjective) - harmonious, measured, ordered, or balanced in character
4. Metamorphosis (noun) -
5. Supercilious (adjective) - coolly and patronizingly haughty
6. Verisimilitude (noun) - the quality or state of being similar to the truth
7. Iconographic (adjective) - representing something by pictures or diagrams

6. Syllables:

1. Indeterminacy (noun) - the quality or state of being indeterminate
2. Ratiocination (noun) - the process of exact thinking

3. Historiography (noun) - the principles, theory, and history of historical writing

4. Infinitesimal (adjective) - immeasurably or incalculably small

7. **Syllables**:

1. Epistemological (adjective) - relating to the study of nature, origin, and limits of human knowledge

Use: merriam-webster.com/ for

pronunciation and definitions of these words.

Part 7

Some Online Resources

ESL/EFL Resources

1. Breaking News English https://breakingnewsenglish.com/

The website has over 2800 English lessons on 7 different levels. You can find recordings there and lots of exercises to practice reading and listening.

2. Learning English with CBC https://www.cbc.ca/learning-english/about-1.4474649

Practice English by watching a video or listening to audio and using an online quiz. You will find the script of the recordings too.

3. Dave's ESL Café https://www.eslcafe.com/resources/grammar-lessons/

Useful source of grammar and vocabulary exercises.

4. Randall's Cyber ESL Listening Lab

https://www.esl-lab.com/intermediate/

Lots of recordings with comprehension questions. If you move your mouse to Listening Activities in the top right corner, you can find easier or more difficult tasks.

5. BBC Learning English https://www.bbc.co.uk/learningenglish/
6. For All Learners Longman Dictionary of Contemporary English Online
   https://www.ldoceonline.com/

Just type the English word in the box at the top, click on the word from menu, and you will get an easy-to-read explanation with examples.

7. British Council

https://learnenglish.britishcouncil.org/

Start with the test to find out your level then go to Getting started and choose a section you want to work on.

8. Activities for ESL Students http://a4esl.org/

Quizzes, tests, exercises and puzzles to help you learn English vocabulary and grammar.

9. English Listening Lesson Library Online http://elllo.org/

ELLLO offers over 2,500 free listening lessons beginner, intermediate and advanced students. You can listen to a recording or watch a video. Then you can do grammar and reading comprehension exercises.

Free online resources

10. University of Lethbridge, English Language Institute Open Educational Resources (mostly focused on listening and speaking): https://eliuleth2018.wixsite.com/open-copy

11. CBC Learning English (archive): https://www.cbc.ca/learning-english

12. BBC Learning English: https://www.bbc.co.uk/learningenglish/english/features/english-at-university; https://www.bbc.co.uk/learningenglish/

13. Voice of America English Learning: https://learningenglish.voanews.com/

14. BC campus, Open Education Resources
    a. English language learning: https://open.bccampus.ca/browse-our-collection/find-open-textbooks/?subject=English+Language
    b. Professional communication: https://open.bccampus.ca/browse-our-collection/find-open-textbooks/?subject=Professional+Communication
    c. Adult basic education English: https://open.bccampus.ca/browse-our-collection/find-open-textbooks/?subject=English
    d. College and university success: https://open.bccampus.ca/browse-our-collection/find-open-textbooks/?subject=College%2FUniversity+Success

15. Coursera: https://www.coursera.org/browse/language-learning/learning-english?languages=en
    a. University of California, Irvine

Academic discussions in English: https://www.coursera.org/learn/academic-discussion-english

Advanced academic speaking and

listening: https://www.coursera.org/specializations/speaklistenenglish

    b. Georgia Tech

i.   English Communication skills: https://www.coursera.org/learn/english-communication-capstone

ii.   Professional speaking: https://www.coursera.org/learn/speak-english-professionally

16. Cambridge Learning English (many activities are free): https://www.cambridgeenglish.org/learning-english/

17. Lesson stream: https://legacy.lessonstream.com/lessons/

18. ESL Games (kids and adults): https://bogglesworldesl.com/esl_games.htm

19. Ted Talks for listening practice: https://www.ted.com/

Made in the USA
Las Vegas, NV
14 December 2023

82817678R00075

dtaymond